KEY A2
Pocket Teaching Guide

Von Jeremy Taylor

Key A2 Pocket Teaching Guide

Verfasser
Jeremy Taylor, Brno

Beratende Mitarbeit
Dietlind Unger, Leipzig

Außenredaktion
Janan Barksdale, Berlin

Verlagsredaktion
Susanne Schütz

Projektleitung
Murdo MacPhail

Illustration (Kopiervorlagen)
Christian Bartz, Berlin; Bettina Kumpe, Braunschweig

Titelbild
Shutterstock (Times Square New York)

Umschlaggestaltung
Klein & Halm Grafikdesign, Berlin

Layout und technische Umsetzung
zweiband.media, Berlin

www.cornelsen.de

Die Internetadressen und -dateien, die in diesem Teaching Guide angegeben sind,
wurden vor Drucklegung geprüft. Der Verlag übernimmt keine Gewähr
für die Aktualität und den Inhalt dieser Adressen und Dateien oder solcher,
die mit ihnen verlinkt sind.

1. Auflage, 1. Druck 2010

Alle Drucke dieser Auflage sind inhaltlich unverändert
und können im Unterricht nebeneinander verwendet werden.

© 2010 Cornelsen Verlag, Berlin

Das Werk und seine Teile sind urheberrechtlich geschützt.
Jede Nutzung in anderen als den gesetzlich zugelassenen Fällen bedarf der vorherigen schriftlichen
Einwilligung des Verlages.
Hinweis zu den §§ 46, 52a UrhG: Weder das Werk noch seine Teile dürfen ohne eine solche Einwilligung
eingescannt und in ein Netzwerk eingestellt oder sonst öffentlich zugänglich gemacht werden.
Dies gilt auch für Intranets von Schulen und sonstigen Bildungseinrichtungen.
Die Kopiervorlagen dürfen für den eigenen Unterrichtsgebrauch in der jeweils benötigten Anzahl
vervielfältigt werden.

Druck: Druckhaus Berlin-Mitte GmbH

ISBN 978-3-06-020099-3

 Inhalt gedruckt auf säurefreiem Papier aus nachhaltiger Forstwirtschaft.

Contents

Introduction & teaching tips	04
Unit 1	18
Unit 2	24
Unit 3	30
Unit 4	36
Journal I	42
Unit 5	44
Unit 6	50
Unit 7	56
Unit 8	62
Journal II	68
Unit 9	70
Unit 10	76
Unit 11	82
Journal III	88
Unit 12	90

Symbols used in this Pocket Teaching Guide

 pairwork activities

 group activities

 CD and track number

 answer key or suggested answers

 photocopiable material

Introduction

Welcome to KEY!

KEY is a new concept. With KEY we want to make it easy for teachers to teach great lessons, and also to make it easy for learners to make fantastic progress and enjoy learning English – and all with a minimum of stress for everyone.

Our 'take and teach' format means you can just pick up the book and teach. All the activities are clearly presented on the page with simple instructions. Each double page spread is one lesson, and each lesson has the right balance of speaking, listening, reading, writing, grammar and vocabulary. You can be sure each lesson contains a variety of interesting practice opportunities for your learners.

One central element of KEY is that in each lesson, your students will talk about themselves, their lives, their opinions, their experience. The English they learn is exactly the English they need to talk about what is most important to them. KEY really is a fully personalized English course.

Of course this Teaching Guide gives you the answers to the activities, but that's not all – you'll also find lots of extra ideas for your lessons.

KEY concept

KEY A2 has 12 units that cover stimulating themes. The clear structure matches the learning needs of adult learners at A2 level.

- Each unit has four related parts – or lessons.
- Lessons A and B introduce the topic and provide basic practice of the new language with a variety of activities.
- Lesson C offers more practice opportunities on the theme, and consolidates the grammar and vocabulary in new and interesting ways.
- Lesson D has lots of quick grammar and vocabulary exercises, together with reading and listening exercises for important skills practice. It's also a great way of measuring progress, and you can use it as handy homework for your students.

In addition to interesting lessons, KEY also offers you and your students regular Journal pages. These colourful, authentic materials have been chosen because they are interesting, relevant and memorable – your students will want to read them and talk about them, even out of class. In fact, we don't think you will be able to stop yourself!

Here are some of the advantages KEY offers you and your students:

- Lots of variety, so students are always interested.
- A range of activity types to suit all sorts of learners.
- KEY verbs, to help students develop their vocabulary and fluency quickly.
- Short and manageable activities that give everybody a sense of achievement.
- Lots of authentic materials from newspapers, magazines and conversations so your students practise real English in real situations.
- Hundreds of oral pairwork activities so that your students use the English they've learnt immediately.
- A strong focus on personalized activities, so students can talk about themselves, their lives and their opinions.
- Grammar activities related to real contexts, so that the new grammar structures are easy to understand and apply.

We hope you all enjoy teaching with KEY!

The KEY authors & editorial team

Teaching tips

In the next few pages we offer a few teaching tips that you may find useful. Teachers with very little teaching experience might like to read these pages carefully. Those teachers with more experience may also like to have a look as there is always something new to learn.

One of the big problems for you as a teacher is how to deal with students of different abilities. For this reason, the first topic for the teaching tips is how to deal with heterogeneous classes.

Getting the most from ... mixed-ability classes

No test that is given to students before joining a new language class will divide the students perfectly – you will not have 25 clones, all with the same level of listening, reading, speaking and writing skills. There is a wide range of activities in KEY and you will find that some students find some tasks easy, while others struggle. While the students are working on an exercise, doing a mill and match etc., you have the opportunity to move around and help the ones who need more help. The Teaching Guide also offers a number of extension exercises which the faster students can do while the weaker ones are finishing the main exercise. Finally, the photocopiables sometimes incorporate a section for slightly higher level students.

Top ten tips for a successful mixed-ability class

1. When arranging groups, try to get a mix of strong and weak students in each group.
2. At times, get the stronger students to help the weaker students.
3. Praise your weaker students for their contributions as their confidence is likely to be shaky.
4. If your weaker students need some extra help, allow the other students to continue with another exercise while you sort out a particular problem. Don't feel that all the students have to be doing the same thing at the same time.
5. While monitoring, try to have a chat with the weaker students to build up their confidence. Don't forget the stronger students may like to be stretched so have a chat with them at a slightly higher level than is normal in the class.
6. Encourage the group to work as a team in their struggle to learn English. This will make the group more cohesive and make things easier for you (and them).
7. When giving homework, consider giving different homework to different students to cope with their different abilities.

8   Enjoy the variety of activities that every unit of KEY offers. If your weaker students find something a little tough, they can be sure that something easier will be just around the corner.
9   If stronger students finish before the others, encourage them to look at Part C of the unit, or they can read the journal material.
10 If a student is much too strong, or much too weak for the group, have a word with the director of studies about the possibility of moving them to a higher or lower group where they will feel more comfortable. This will also be better for the others in the group who won't feel discouraged by someone much better than they are – or feel sorry for someone who is much weaker than they are.

Getting the most from ... speaking tasks

In KEY A2 there are many different kinds of speaking activities as this is the skill that most students want to improve. You will find:

- **Pairwork – problem solving:** Definitely two heads are better than one when it comes to solving a problem.
- **Pairwork – exchanging views:** The KEY exercises are designed so that the students can exchange views on a wide variety of topics – and also use the target grammar and vocabulary frequently and painlessly.
- **Pairwork – answer checking:** Once students have completed an exercise it makes a lot of sense to check their answers with their partner. If there are any discrepancies, they have time to look again.
- **Group work – prioritizing exercises:** There are many exercises in KEY in which the students have to prioritize something. This could be the order in which they organize a holiday or the most important qualities for friendship. The important thing about such exercises is that there is no correct answer: the students themselves will decide the order, and the answer that they come up with is of secondary importance compared to the discussion that went on to produce the answer.
- **Group work – brainstorming:** This is a great opportunity for your students to pool their resources and come up with some creative ideas. It might be a meal for a visitor from another country or it could be things to do on a wet Saturday afternoon but encourage them to be as creative as possible.
- **Group work – sharing responses:** In many exercises, once the exercise has been done in pairs, the students then share these responses within a group. Many students find this recycling of their ideas very useful as it builds up their confidence.

Top ten tips for a good speaking activity

1. Make sure the students know what to do before they start the speaking activity. Rather than repeating the instructions twice, you may like to get one of your students to reiterate the instructions.
2. Don't ask the question: *Do you understand what to do?* as it is unlikely a student who doesn't understand what to do will have the confidence to say so.
3. You may like to model the interaction before the students all start talking. This is particularly useful for an activity like 'find someone who' with which some students may not be familiar.
4. Make sure that the students are talking (a lot) more than you.
5. If there is an activity in which the whole class is involved, e. g. asking each other for information, feel free to join in. The students will benefit from your model answers, and you can be part of the buzz of a successful class.
6. In general, encourage fluency rather than accuracy. After the activity you make like to look at some of the errors being made, particularly if it involved the target structure.
7. When you talk to your students, talk as naturally as possible. Ask *Have you ever been to Brazil?* as though you genuinely want to know the answer, rather than the question being just another example of the present perfect.
8. Encourage your students to talk to a variety of partners. Practice makes perfect and if they can ask (and answer) their questions ten times, then it will be better than asking and answering just once.
9. Many of the exercises in KEY get the students to talk about their own experiences and opinions. This allows the students to find out more about each other and keeps an activity fresh.
10. Make sure you conclude the activity before the students run out of ideas. Though originally from the world of show business, the rule 'stop while the audience wants more' is good advice in the classroom as well. A lively and fun discussion may run for 3-4 minutes but if you try to let it run for 10 minutes then you will get some bored students. Given the great variety in KEY, your students can be sure that it won't be long before they are given the opportunity to have another enthusiastic discussion!

Getting the most from ... listening tasks

Listening tasks are vital for your students to hear a great variety of English. BBC English is not the only English in the world and in KEY your students will be exposed to a wide variety of accents and English spoken by people of different ages.

In KEY you will find lots of listening comprehension exercises and they are always supported with an activity for the students to do while listening. It is always a good idea to discuss the recording before you play it, by saying, for example: *We're going to hear an interview between a television producer and two people who want to be on a reality TV show. What kind of questions do you think he will ask?* If you do this kind of pre-listening task, your students will be better prepared for when they hear the dialogue. If your students look puzzled at the end, offer to play it again. Before you do, get them to discuss the answers that they did get.

Many of the recordings in KEY have more than one exercise. This will mean your students will hear the recording more than once. The more often they hear it, the easier it is for them to understand it.

Top ten tips for a good listening exercise

1. Get the CD ready to play before the class begins.
2. Introduce the topic of the listening to whet your students' appetite for the subject.
3. Give the students time to read the exercise before you play the recording.
4. Expect to play the recording more than once.
5. Teach your students the phrase: *Could you play that again, please?*
6. Sit still and listen to the recording with the students. Don't distract them.
7. If your students are struggling, stop the recording a few times to give them time to complete the exercise.
8. Another way to help struggling students is to allow them to look at the transcripts – though try not to encourage this for everyone.
9. If the acoustics are poor in the classroom, get your students to come closer to the CD player.
10. After the recording, get your students to discuss the answers to the exercise in pairs or small groups.

Getting the most from ... reading tasks

Reading is a very important skill and there is plenty of reading practice throughout the book. However you won't find many long passages as reading a passage for more than a few minutes does not give rise to a lively classroom atmosphere that your students will enjoy.

One problem that some students have with reading in a foreign language is that they want to understand every word. They sit with a difficult text and stop every sentence to look up the meaning of a word (or three) that they don't know, or perhaps just to check that they have understood the word correctly. It is a good idea to encourage your students to look at the context in which a word appears and have a good guess at the meaning. Secondly, do they really need to know the word to understand the text? Often it is better for them to keep reading and not worry about every word that is unfamiliar.

Reading is a great way to introduce new vocabulary and structures to students and the more they read, the more frequently they will come across these new words, and the better their English will become.

KEY is quite special in that there are regular journal pages which your students can read just for pleasure.

Getting the most from ... the Journals

The Journals are a special part of KEY and it is entirely up to you (and your students) how you use the material found there. One possibility is to simply say *Enjoy*! and let your students browse through the journal when they have a free moment and look at the articles that they find intrinsically interesting. This is particularly useful if you have a heterogeneous class and some students need some extra 'stretching'. The Journals are the prefect answer to this. They contain language and structures that may be new to the student but the combination of strong visuals and intrinsic interest should mean that your students will want to get as much as they can from the articles.

Another way to use the journals (especially Journal I and II) is to bridge the gap between semesters. During this time away from weekly lessons, some students might feel their English start slipping as they don't get the opportunity to practise. The Journals are an ideal way for your students to keep their English alive during those lonely weeks between English courses.

Having said all that, we are also aware that some teachers (and some students) might want to use some of the journal material in class and prefer a little more guidance in doing so. In this Teaching Guide you will find some tips as to how you might want to exploit the journals with your students.

Top ten tips for working with the journal pages

1 After students have read a story, do a dictation with one part of it. You can either make a small number of changes as you dictate while the students try to remember the original, or you ask them to work in pairs to recall what the next part was.

2. Ask students to complete a tic-tac-toe grid and put nine key words or phrases from the text in the nine squares. Then they compare what they chose and see who has the same, and discuss any differences. They can use the grids to play tic-tac-toe where they can only 'win the square' if they make a correct sentence with the word.
3. Ask pairs to summarize the page in one line of not more than 15 words. Again, ask pairs to compare and vote on the best.
4. Tell students to read the text, then test one another on what they remember. One takes the role of questioner and the other tries to answer from memory.
5. Give pairs five minutes to re-read the page and make five collections of words from it. Examples could be: verbs, adjectives, numbers, words ending with s, prepositions. Then, using the collections, see how much of the text they can recall.
6. All the journal pages have strong visuals. You can ask pairs to concentrate on the visuals for one minute, then you ask a number of testing questions, e.g.: *How many red objects were there in the picture? Was the sky cloudy or not? Was the man wearing jeans or shorts?* You could then ask pairs to do the same.
7. Pairs read the whole journal and then vote on the most interesting/unusual/shocking/memorable/colourful page.
8. Give pairs a list of grammar items that occurred in recent units to look for, e.g. uncountable nouns, irregular plurals, expressions with key verbs, past tenses or modal verbs.
9. Pairs imagine what happened immediately before and after each picture and discuss their stories.
10. Pairs rewrite one part of one page of the journal as a dialogue, then read the dialogue to the class.

Getting the most from … working with photos

KEY is full of some excellent photos and these can be used in many different ways. Often they help to focus the students' attention on a particular subject, holidays, food, emotions etc. There are also many exercises which involve the students looking at the photos – which is good for your visual learners. A fun game to play with your students is to choose a photo from KEY at random. The students can ask questions to find out what is on the photo, but you can only answer with yes or no. Once you have played it, you can get your students to play the same game in groups.

The photos also allow you to stretch the stronger students in a heterogeneous group, for example by extending vocabulary: *So, Beate, what's the name of the thing that the man is wearing to stop his trousers falling down?* (*I think it is a belt.*)

Getting the most from ... the photocopiables

There are a total of 24 photocopiables in the KEY package which complement the exercises in the coursebook. You will find a wide range of activities, and the photocopiables themselves can be used in many different ways. Some groups of students might enjoy the anarchic approach of running around the classroom, trying to match up various parts of a sentence. Other groups may prefer to do the same exercise sitting around a table in quiet discussion with their fellow students. You know your students best, so you decide how best to exploit the material that is available. It is a good idea to familiarize yourself with the photocopiables (and the advice in the Teaching Guide) before using them. The following overview can serve as a useful checklist.

Photocopiable	Good for ...	Your notes
1 Unit 1 Part A Speed friendship!	Talking about yourself, likes & dislikes	
2 Unit 1 Part C Wales – facts & figures	Exchanging facts and figures	
3 Unit 2 Part B Can you help me, please?	Giving advice	
4 Unit 2 Part A Present continuous / simple present	Contrasting present continuous & simple present	
5 Unit 3 Part A Adjectives	Adjectives	
6 Unit 3 Part B Past continuous & simple past	Contrasting past continuous & simple past	
7 Unit 4 Part B Let's get down to work	Job titles (to be used with exercise 1)	
8 Unit 4 Part C The professionals & their equipment	Vocabulary work on job titles & things people need to do their work	
9 Unit 5 Part A A mix up at the restaurant	Vocabulary work on food items	
10 Unit 5 Part B A new special day	Inventing a new special day	

11 Unit 6 Part A What are you doing on …?	Making arrangements	
12 Unit 6 Part C Boost your vocabulary!	Crossword puzzle on vocabulary from Unit 6	
13 Unit 7 Part A I have … but I haven't …	Present perfect	
14 Unit 7 Part B Have you done it yet?	Present perfect with *already* & *yet*	
15 Unit 8 Part A Too … and not … enough	*Too … and not … enough*	
16 Unit 8 Part B *I used to … but now …*	*Used to*	
17 Unit 9 Part B Can you help me? (Help! Help! cards)	Vocabulary work on appliances and devices, offering help	
18 Unit 9 Part B (Gadget cards)	See above.	
19 Unit 10 Part A Until …	Making sentences with *until*	
20 Unit 10 Part B What will I need …?	*Will*-future & sports equipment	
21 Unit 11 Part A Mr and Mrs Poor	Justifying purchases	
22 Unit 11 Part B Giving it all away	Inventing charities, making short presentations	
23 Unit 11 Part C Lights, camera, action!	Shopping role-plays as scenes from films	
24 Unit 12 Part B Looking back	Writing short stories and dialogues	

Getting the most from … classroom set ups

You may not have a choice in this as the tables may be screwed to the floor. But, if you do have a choice, you may like to arrange your students in small groups around a table so that they can carry out pairwork and group work easily. At times you may like get your students to sit in a large horseshoe so that everyone can see everyone else. Of course, the set up that you use will depend on the facilities available but in KEY there are a variety of different activities and sometimes moving the furniture around will make the task more effective.

Even if your furniture is fixed, there is no good reason why your students should work with the same people every minute of every lesson. It is refreshing for them to get up, move around and then work with a new partner or group.

Top ten tips for a mixing up groups

1. Tell the group: *Everyone who is wearing a ring (or wearing something blue or wearing black shoes), change places!*
   Get your students to arrange themselves in order of their birthdays (not date of birth!).
3. Get your students to arrange themselves alphabetically.
4. Write famous couples on separate pieces of paper. Hand out the pieces. The students then have to find their partner: *Excuse me, are you Delilah? (Yes, Samson!)* They now have a new person to work with.
5. Write questions and answers on separate pieces of paper and hand them out. The students then have to find their partner: *Do you know when the last people walked on the moon? (Yes, it was 1972!)* They now have a new person to work with.
6. Write numbers on separate pieces of paper and hand them out. The students then have to find their partner: *Excuse me, is your number 390? (No, sorry. I have 319.)* They keep going until they find the person with the same number.
7. If your students are sitting in a horseshoe, simply move one person from one end of the horseshoe, to the other. In that way, everyone has a new partner.
8. Write A, B and C on a number of pieces of paper. The students take one each and then form three groups of As, Bs and Cs. (Clearly, if you want more groups, you can add more letters.)
9. Get your students to arrange themselves according to their height.
10. Get your students to sit next to someone that they don't know very well.

Getting the most from ... feedback sessions

In KEY there are many exercises in which your students work in groups. It is not possible to monitor all groups all the time but a good feedback session will allow you to discover whether the students have completed the task, whether there are any outstanding problems that need to be addressed and whether the group needs more practice of the target structure or whether they are ready to move on.

Introduction & teaching tips

Top ten tips for a good feedback session

1. Make sure that all your students listen to other groups during a feedback session.
2. Ask some checking questions to make sure everyone is listening. (For example: *Which of Sabine's recipes did you like most?*)
3. You don't have to get feedback from every group, after every activity.
4. Make sure that everyone gets a chance to give some feedback, but don't put pressure on the shy or weaker students.
5. Show genuine interest in their answers: *You went to Kenya on holiday? Wow, what was it like?*
6. Try to avoid giving your students the opportunity to answer with just *yes* or *no*. Compare: *Did you have a good time in Majorca?* with *Tell me some of the things you saw in Majorca.*
7. Don't always take the answer from your best students. Try to give the others a chance.
8. If a query comes up in the feedback session, you may want to deal with it straight away. If you think it might take longer, ask the student to make a note of the query so that you can discuss it later.
9. If someone asks you a question and you don't know the answer, admit it, and compliment them on asking such a good question. Make a note of it and get back to the student next lesson.
10. When someone gives you an answer, don't always tell them if it is right or wrong, but ask the opinion of the other students. This makes sure that the students listen to each other's answers, and also enables a healthy debate about the answer.

Getting the most from ... the Homestudy sections

At the end of each unit there is the Homestudy section (Part D). Here you will find excellent consolidation material, which the students can do after each Part (A, B and C) or they can do it all together at the end of the unit. Or, if they are too busy, there is no obligation for them to do it at all (though we don't want to encourage that!).

The students can self correct as there is an answer key at the back of the book. While Part D is intended for homestudy, there is no reason why you can't use some of the exercises in your classes. Especially in heterogeneous classes, you could have the stronger students do, for example, one of the writing exercises while the others are busy with something else. Similarly, weaker students could benefit from doing some of Part D while working together with a partner, rather than on their own back at home.

Last but not least, special attention should be drawn to the listening exercises in the Homestudy section. They are a rich source of natural language and could benefit by more exploitation than provided in the self-study exercises. Have a listen and feel free to integrate one or two in your lesson.

However you choose to use it, the homestudy section is a useful resource which gives your students extra practice of the structures and language covered in earlier parts of the unit.

Getting the most from … the portfolio pages

You'll notice as you flip through the book, that Parts C and D of Unit 12 are different than in the rest of the book. In Part C there is a pinboard with 'Can you …?' questions and in Part D you'll find the Portfolio pages.

The pinboard in Part C is closely connected to the tasks stipulated by the can-do statements in Part D (see below). The photographs and notes on the pinboard have been carefully selected to reflect the unit contents and are supported by the three sets of 'can you?' questions (colour-coded to match the three semesters of the book). The visuals and questions together can be used as a springboard for revision and discussion, either at the end of each unit or at the end of a semester, and offer even those teachers who choose not to use the Portfolio pages a creative and informal way to revise much of the material covered in the book.

Part D offers a more formalized way of dealing with (and covering) can-do statements. The portfolio pages can be used to keep track of students' progress and to check whether they have reached the learning targets (unit aims).The set-up is easy. Each unit has three can-do statements that reflect that units' contents and aims, both thematically and grammatically. Should the students feel they need more help with a particular area, they can look at the pages in the Units or Grammar section indicated in the table. Underneath each unit's can-do statements, there is a task that invites the students to actually show what they can do – using visuals either on the pinboard or in the units.

Learning strategies on the right of each chart offer some additional help to the learner, but are not actually related to the units' contents or aims.

Ideally, the students should refer to the Portfolio pages upon completion of each unit. They can look at the can-do statements and do the practical task. If the students require further help, they can follow the links to parts of the book where they can find out more about a particular language area.

It is useful for the students if the Portfolio pages can be looked at in class time. This will allow your students to ask you for help – if such help is needed. Once they have filled in the Portfolio pages for a couple of units, they may feel confident enough to be able to fill it in themselves in their own time.

At the end of unit 1 your students should:
- have revised the simple present including of *to be* and *to have (got)*.
- have practised meeting and greeting.
- be able to use pronouns and possessive pronouns effectively.
- know a range of countries and the corresponding nationalities.
- have had lots of practice of making questions.
- be able to give personal information.

A Great to see you again! coursebook pages 10–11

1 A nice warm-up activity to get the students out of their chairs. Encourage them to talk to people they have not met before. In the second part you don't need to hear from everyone. Just ask two or three people for the most interesting information that they found out

2 A quick reading exercise for your students as a quick revision of the verb *to be*.

    Thursday night is bowling night.

In the second part of the exercise, the students have to underline all the forms of *to be* in the email and then compare notes with a partner.

I'm back home   Kathy and Pete are
It's bowling night!   they're so lucky
today's Thursday.   Our team's very small

3 This is a fun exercise for you and your students. Feel free to make as many mistakes as you want – as long as the students are still enjoying it.

4 Your students will hear Valerie and Ben greeting each other at the bowling club. Before listening, you could get your students to fill in the three gaps with the words in the box at the bottom. Have a quick discussion as to which words could go in the gaps.

    1 good, great, nice   2 bad   3 fine, good

(Many British people now use *I'm good* in response to *How are you?* though some people see this as incorrect.)

1.2 Then play the recording. What words do they actually use?

    1 great   2 bad   3 fine

5 **1.3** The listening continues. Give your students a few moments to read the sentences before you start the recording. You may want to stop the recording a few times, and play it again if your students need more help.

    1 ✓   4 No, just an old friend.
    2 No. He prefers peace and quiet.   5 ✓
    3 No. He's from Brazil.   6 ✓

6 Students select phrases you can use when meeting people for the first time. Make sure they understand that the other phrases can be used to greet people they already know.

    ✓   2 Very nice to meet you.
    ✓   3 I don't think we've met before.
    ✓   5 It's a pleasure to meet you.
    ✓   7 How do you do? (Only used by some people in very formal situations. The reply is the same: *How do you do?*)

In the second part of the exercise, students stand up and meet and greet each other. You should join in this exercise. Make sure students use appropriate phrases for people they know and for new people that they have not met before.

> Use **photocopiable 1** to get your students to practise asking and answering questions.
>
> - Make enough copies so that each student in your class has a card. Cut out the cards.
> - Explain to the students that they are going to have a 'speed friendship' activity – a bit like speed dating. Give them each cards with information about 'their' personalities. Have them add fictional names to the cards.
> - Get them to sit in pairs. Before they start, you might like to review the questions they'll need: *What's your name? What kinds of things do/don't you like?* etc.
> - Each pair has just two minutes to ask as many questions as they can based on the information on the cards. (If your students need more time, you could extend this but don't let them get bored.) Then they move on to the next person.
> - They should make brief notes about the people they meet.
> - After they have met four or five people, get them to decide which one person they would like to be friends with – and why.

7 A quick matching exercise, matching the pronouns with the possessive pronouns.

    1 F   2 D   3 G   4 B   5 C   6 A   7 E

Unit 1 Part A

8 A simple gapfill exercise using the pronouns and possessive pronouns from exercise 7. Get your students to work in pairs for this one.

    1 I, my   3 I, we, our
    2 She, her, his   4 They, their

9 A final bit of revision – countries and the corresponding nationalities. The following are the countries that have cropped up in Part A. Students can come up with plenty more in the second part of the exercise.

    Italy – Italian   Thailand – Thai
    Mongolia – Mongolian   Denmark – Danish
    Brazil – Brazilian   Peru – Peruvian
    Wales – Welsh

B That's me!

coursebook pages 12–13

1 A warm-up activity which you may like to model for your students before they try it in pairs or small groups. Don't choose any really obscure things and try to lead your students to the answers.

2 A reading exercise for your students about Madhu Baldwin from Nottingham. If your students are slow readers, you could take it section by section and ask them simple questions about the text.

    1/4   It takes her a quarter of an hour to cycle to work.
    1/2   There's a park half a mile from where Madhu lives.
    21   is the number of seats in the cinema where she works.
    25   is the house number of the building where she works.
    1997   is the year she moved to Hockley.

3 A quick review of the reading passage should be enough for your students to find things in common with Madhu and things that are different. The review of the simple present may be useful to students and for more information they can have a look at page 135.

4 Simple revision allowing for greater student talking time. Make sure you move around and monitor. Direct students who are still struggling with the structure to the grammar box.

    1 Where do you live?
    2 What do you do in the evening?
    3 How many pets do you have? Or How many pets have you got?
    4 What is your favourite part of town?
    5 How far is it (not it is) to the nearest cinema?
    6 Who else in the class lives close to you?

As they did earlier with the Madhu interview, they now find some things in common and some things that are different with their classmates.

5 **1.4** Your students will hear a radio announcement about Nottingham and what it has to offer. They should fill in the data in the table and then, in the second part, work with a partner to add information about their own town, neighbourhood or region.

Number of residents	300,000
shopping	Modern shopping centres and traditional markets
Culture and nightlife	Art galleries, museums and theatres
	Hundreds of bars, nightclubs and pubs
Nature and sport	Sherwood Forest only 25 minutes away
	Horse riding and golf.
Local festivals and specialities	Goose fair in October
	Mushy peas and mint sauce

6 This can be a fun activity, particularly if you have a lively, outgoing class. Give them time to prepare their texts – which can then be pinned up for others to read.

> **Extension activity:** Once they have written about a place, they shouldn't find it too hard to give a short presentation. Tell them that a travel company is looking for new locations and they should present the town they have chosen in just one minute, rather like a TV commercial. Again, give them time to prepare and help them with any phrases they need. eir sentences for the whole class.

7 **1.5** A listening exercise. Your students will hear personal details of a woman who calls a special service in Nottingham. You may need to stop the recording to give them time to write the information down.

surname	Leisser
first name	Brenda
telephone	0115 988 1947
home address	(not given)
postal code	(not given)
email address	brenda.leisser@gingsters.com
Interests	Sporting events, family activities

8 Some very important practice at the end: exchanging telephone numbers and e-mail addresses. Make sure they read the box on the right of the page before they start.

Unit 1 Part B

C That's pretty unusual

coursebook pages 14–15

1 A quick 'find someone who' activity to get the students out of their chairs. Encourage them to talk to as many different people as possible. In the feedback session, you don't need to hear from everyone. Just ask two or three people for the most interesting information that they found out.

2 **1.6** Your students discuss which of the three famous people are most likely to fit each of the six descriptions. They then listen a recording which will give them the answers.

Graf	2, 4
Obama	2, 3, 5
Depp	1, 6

3 A nice exercise for students to practise question words, with some speaking practice as follow up.

1 Who/Where   4 What
2 Where   5 How/Where
3 Which   6 Where/How/Why

> **Extension activity:** The students write questions about a famous person that they like (or at least someone they know a lot about. They then ask the questions in small groups.

4 The first part of this exercise shouldn't take too long, but you might need to help some students with writing their profiles.

 When you read out the profiles, try not to give the most obvious piece of information first so that the students have to think a bit.

> Use **photocopiable 2** to give students some practice exchanging facts and figures as well as some interesting information about Wales.
>
> - Make copies (one sheet per pair of students) and cut the sheets in half.
> - Have students work in pairs and give each of them one of the halves. Tell them not to show each other their information.
> - Students take it in turns to ask each other about the missing information and to complete the gaps.
> - After they have exchanged all their information, they can compare results.

5 **Key verbs: be and have (got).** In British English it is common to ask: *Have you got a bicycle?* whereas Americans would ask: *Do you have a bicycle?* The American form is used in Britain though it is rare to hear the British form in America. Get your students to work together on this one. (*Note that a man is blond but a woman is blonde. A rare case of different adjectives for men and women in English.)

> **be** blond(e)*, divorced, hungry, retired, lucky, single, Swiss
> **be at** a friend's house, school
> **be in** Austria, a classroom, a friend's house, a garden, a school, a shop
> **be on** holiday, time
> **have (got)** brown hair, green eyes

6 A reading text with gapfill. Your students will read a text about a rare phenomenon, an Englishman who can speak foreign languages!

> 1 can't speak/don't speak
> 2 speaks/can speak
> 3 doesn't see
> 4 lives
> 5 runs
> 6 play
> 7 eats
> 8 weighs
> 9 have
> 10 holds
> 11 hasn't got/doesn't have

7 The final exercise is a quiz about languages and numbers. Your students shouldn't be expected to get the right answers but they should make educated guesses. (And get some practice saying different types of numbers.) The answers can be found on page 130.

At the end of unit 2 your students should:
- have practised the simple present and the present continuous.
- have practised a range of adverbs of frequency.
- have talked about abilities and routines.
- have discussed modern ways of keeping in touch.
- be able to make polite requests.

A Yes, I can

coursebook pages 18–19

1 Find people who ... A nice warm-up activity to get people moving around, formulating and asking questions. Encourage your students to talk to as many different people as possible. In the feedback session, just ask for the most interesting thing they found out, rather than all the information.

2 Reality TV shows are very popular in the UK. Let your students **discuss** in small groups whether they like them or not – or what other kinds of programmes they like.

3 A simple matching exercise. There are enough clues in the photos that your students shouldn't struggle with this one.

    A Britain's got Talent
    B Castaway
    C Come Dine with Me!

4 A vocabulary exercise to check your students' understanding of the text.

    1 islands   4 complete
    2 hut   5 talented
    3 nasty

5 This should be a fun exercise. Give your students some time to think of some good questions for you. And remember – you don't have to tell the truth!

6 **1.8** A listening comprehension giving your students plenty of opportunity to hear adverbs of frequency in context.

    1 Kim – with her ex-husband. Daniel plays, but only occasionally.
    2 She goes running.
    3 Every Monday, and sometimes on Thursday.
    4 Twice a week

5 Yes, she does, but Daniel never does. (cook)
   6 Kim. DIY is 'not Daniel's thing'. (He doesn't like it.)

Students might come up with the following additional information about Daniel and Kim:

> Kim is 32, she's a vet from Luton, is divorced, has two children. She can't sew, can cook nice dinners and does a lot of DIY.
>
> Daniel is 25, single and a DJ from Blackburn in Lancashire. He goes clubbing, doesn't have a garden, can't cook and has problems putting up IKEA furniture.

Extension activity: In groups, the students interview each other to see who would be the best candidate for Castaway. In the feedback session they can explain who they chose, and what qualities the person has which makes them a suitable candidate for Castaway.

7 While the order of some of the adverbs of frequency can be debated, it should be roughly as follows. (If students need more help, they can have a look at page 143.)

> C – B – G – F – D – H – A – E
> (never – hardly ever – occasionally – sometimes – as often as I can – quite often – regularly – always)

Encourage your students to be creative with their choice of sentences. You could turn it into a game in which the students read out their sentences but say 'blank' in place of the adverb of frequency (e.g. *I 'blank' ride my bike to work*). The other students have to think of an appropriate adverb (*never? occasionally?*).

8 More practice of adverbs of frequency – this time in pairs. Show plenty of interest in the feedback session to make the language as natural as possible.

9 **1.9** A The focus of this Sounds good exercise is on voiced and unvoiced word endings. The students also have the opportunity to hear the words in context (track 10).

> 1 surf   3 ice   5 live   7 hid
> 2 bag   4 rope   6 dock   8 cap

10 A vocabulary-boosting exercise. Encourage your students to be creative. You might want to draw the spider diagrams on the board so that they can add their ideas after a brainstorming session.

11 **Class survey.** A nice way to recycle the language from part A. There should be lots of noise as your students discuss how often they do things. Plenty of humour there as the women ask the men how often they wear high heels, etc.

Unit 2 Part A

B What's going on?

coursebook pages 20–21

1 How do you keep in touch? This warmer gets people moving around and discussing how we communicate nowadays. Get the students to pool their results in small groups before the feedback session.

2 A quick reading exercise for your students – divide them into As and Bs. Can they answer their partner's questions without looking at the text again?

	Zack	Neil
lives	in Manchester	in New York
friends live	in Manchester	abroad (many of them)
stays in touch	by phone, text, email and a Facebook page	by email and twitter

3 A vocabulary exercise which shouldn't be too difficult for your students. It is possible that some of your students will not be familiar with Twitter. Ask those that are familiar to explain briefly how it works.

1 son, steps
2 wine, sun
3 game
4 food
5 couch, single

4 Students unscramble sentences, which are all in the present continuous. You can get your students to work together on this one.

A2 Jill and her friends are sitting on the balcony.   in (extra word)
B3 Barry is watching a hockey game.   are
C5 Marsha is enjoying some new music.   am
D1 Laura is filming her young child.   on
E4 Bob is trying to find a good restaurant.   not

5 A fun way to practise the present continuous by completing tweets.

Model answers:

1 … are lying next to a stream and having a picnic.
2 …'m dancing on my seat!
3 … is singing 'We will rock you' completely out of tune.
4 … are leaving for the pub!

6 Some vocabulary preparation work for exercise 7 (listening).

1 Asking for help
2 Finding out about the problem
3 Saying yes
4 Saying no

7 **1.11** A listening comprehension. Your students will hear a dialogue between Paul and Ned. Which phrases from exercise 6 do they hear?

I hope you can help me out.
Sure.
So, what's wrong?
Can I borrow your truck, please?
I'm sorry but you can't actually.

Play the recording again. This time the students have to answer four questions.

1 He's standing outside an antique shop.
2 They are closing down today.
3 He's trying to fix his truck.
4 Paul can fix Ned's truck. Ned can lend Paul the truck to move his jukebox.

8 A nice way to recycle the language from part B. The students need to ask a favour – and the other students have to offer their help or come up with excuses.

Model excuses for the first three:

1 I'm sorry, but I have very bad hay fever.
2 I'm afraid not, I don't have a clue about cars.
3 Well that's a bit difficult. I only know how to say 'Je t'aime!'

> Use **photocopiable 3** to practise asking for and offering help or advice.
>
> - Make a copy and cut out the cards. (There are 24 cards in all so you might need more if you have a big class.)
> - Explain to the students that they are going to help each other with their 'problems' and they should get as much advice as they can from their group. Some people will be helpful, others may have excuses for why they can't help. If necessary, review phrases from page 19 for offering help and making excuses.
> - Put students in groups of 3-4 and give each student two to three cards. Students take turns reading out the cards and the other students respond with advice or excuses. The person with the best advice or excuse 'earns' the problem card. (The person with the problem is the judge.) The group member with the most cards at the end of the game 'wins'.
> - In the feedback session the students can relate the most useful piece of advice, the worst excuse, the funniest answer, etc.

C Anybody up for it?

coursebook pages 22-23

1 A quick warm-up exercise to get your students thinking about different locations and the adjectives which can describe them. There is plenty of room for flexible answers here as your students will hopefully have different views on different places.

> Suggested answers:
> theatres: noisy, old, dirty, crowded, stuffy
> concert halls: lively, noisy, old, crowded, smoky, stuffy
> town halls: relaxing, quiet, interesting, old
> town squares: lively, noisy, interesting, old, dirty, crowded
> city parks: soothing, relaxing, quiet, interesting, old,
> shopping centres/malls: noisy, crowded, boring
> pubs: lively, noisy, interesting, old, stuffy
> cafés: relaxing, interesting, lively, quiet

2 Describing pictures. Get your students to work in small groups for this one. You may have to help them with the word *pillow*.

3 Reading comprehension exercise. Hopefully your students can think of some local attractions that fit the descriptions.

> 1 True   5 False
> 2 True   6 True
> 3 False   7 True
> 4 False   8 False

4 **1.12** Listening comprehension. Students hear three people talk to Juliette.

> ✓ to use her mobile phone
> ✓ to know what time it is
> ✓ to find out how to get somewhere

Students then have to complete the sentences with verbs in the simple present or present continuous.

> Suggested answers:
> 1 wants   4 have
> 2 is looking   5 is going
> 3 is looking   6 run, 's not/isn't, don't cost

Unit 2 Part C

5 **Key verb: run.** Once the students have done the exercise, you can extend it by asking, for example, what else you can run out of (*time, milk, beer, patience* etc.).

1 The pen is running out of ink.
2 She runs the marathon every year.
3 Janet is running for a bus.
4 Mary and Paul often run into one other.
5 We never run out of ideas.

6 In this exercise there is the opportunity for the students to talk about their own experiences. Get the students to discuss in groups before you bring it all together in a feedback session. Note that you might need to explain what a scavenger hunt is (= a game in which players have to find objects, or *Schnitzeljagd*).

In part 2, it could be fun to do a role-play with some students being the foreign tourists and some being the helpful locals. Give them some time to prepare: the 'foreigners' can prepare some questions, the locals can prepare some suggestions.

7 **And finally ...** The students have to do a little bit of work, choosing the correct tense, before asking each other the questions.

> Use **photocopiable 4** give your students some more practice with simple present and present continuous.
>
> - Cut out the cards and hand them out, one per person.
> - Explain that this is a speaking exercise, so the students mustn't look at each other's cards.
> - Students mill around and read their sentence halves to each other until they find a match. (Both people should read their part; even if they don't match, the object is to practise their English, not just match up the sentences.)
> - Once the students find their match, they can sit down (or take new cards – if there are some extras – and do another round).
> - During the feedback session, you can have some pairs read out their complete sentences.
>
> This is a lively activity and should provide some amusing answers.

3

At the end of unit 3 your students should:
- be comfortable about talking about the past, including using irregular past tense forms and the past continuous.
- have a wider range of adjectives (not everything is *nice* or *good*).
- be able to talk about their experiences (including what they did on holiday) and tell stories.
- be able to react appropriately when other people tell stories or give news.

A Strange but true
coursebook pages 26–27

1 A quick warm-up exercise to get students to think about the past and to use the past tense form of the verb *to be*. In weaker classes you could model the activity first by giving the students a specific time (e. g. *Monday evening*) and having them ask *you* questions: *Were you at home? (No, but I was in a building.) Was it a classroom? (No, …)*

Make sure students understand that 'last night' refers to the evening as well. They might be embarrassed if they think they are talking about *letzte Nacht*.

2 **Quick check.** Students match up some common verbs with their irregular past forms.

fall – fell	know – knew	swim – swam	write – wrote
feel – felt	meet – met	wear – wore	
get – got	speak – spoke	win – won	

3 Make sure students know what a blog is (web + log) before reading the text. Ask: *Do you write one? Do you read other people's blogs? What are they about?*

> **Extra activity:** To encourage your students to use the target structure naturally, you can get them to interview each other using the ten items below the instructions. In the feedback session, ask students for the most interesting facts they found out about each other, e. g. *Karin ate lobster in California on her honeymoon!* After you have asked two or three people, do a little test to see who was listening: *Who ate lobster in California? Who saw a penguin at London Zoo?*

- ✓ went to a museum
- ✓ got stuck in a lift
- ✓ watched a play
- ✓ had some beer

Unit 3 Part A

4 A nice bit of revision here. Note that learners often mix up *Tuesday* and *Thursday*.

⚬ on Tuesday – at a museum
on Wednesday – at a famous home and an unusual restaurant
on Thursday – at a nature reserve
on Friday – on the highway

5 Can the students see which verbs are in the *-ied* column? (The ones ending in a consonant +y.)

Regular			Irregular
-d	-ed	-ied	–
stared, arrived	stayed, visited	tried, hurried	had, was/were, went, saw, spent

6 Encourage students to discuss the answers with their neighbours. Early finishers could write their own comment on Pamela's blog (e. g. perhaps a question about something she wrote).

⚬ 1 stayed   4 didn't have   7 wasn't
2 were   5 went   8 enjoyed
3 spent   6 didn't see   9 Did (you) try

7 **Odd one out.** Students can work alone or in pairs to find the adjectives that don't fit.

⚬ Suggested answers:
1 awesome – as the others refer to the size of something.
2 wild – as the others refer to food.
3 great – as the others are all negative.
4 famous – as the others refer to the price of something.
5 embarrassed – as the others are all positive.

Encourage students to be creative in the second part of the exercise. You might even want to 'give points' to the pair who come up with the most original adjectives.

⚬ Suggested answers:
A great, exciting, green, pleasant, historic city. A huge and scary city.
An exciting, brilliant night out. An expensive night out.
Tasty, delicious, exotic food. Dull, bland, tasteless food.
A great, well-equipped, clean, luxury hotel. A friendly, cheap hotel.

> 🔑 Use **photocopiable 5** to give your students more practice using adjectives creatively.
>
> - Students work first in group of 3-4. Make one copy for each group and cut out the cards.
> - Hand out a set of adjective cards to each group and have students discuss how they would use the adjectives in a sentence.
> - Have a quick feedback session, then have students put the adjective cards aside.
> - Now distribute the sentence cards, one or more per person.
> - Get the students to move around the room, reading their sentence to their fellow students, who should provide a suitable adjective at the end. They should remember some of the adjectives they have just looked at.
> - Finally, back in their groups of 3-4, they can match up all of the adjectives with all of the sentences.

8 👥 This is a popular topic for students and they should be able to talk about their last holiday without much trouble. Make sure that you mingle and ask a few questions to encourage the students if they seem to be struggling.

B What were you doing? coursebook pages 28-29

1 A nice little warm-up exercise on the way to refer to the time (of day). You might want to remind students of the difference between German and English when we say *half seven*. I have missed quite a few dates thanks to that misunderstanding!

🔑
- 7.15 am – in the morning
- 1.15 pm – in the early afternoon
- 7.35 pm – in the evening
- 10.30 pm – at night
- 11.45 am – just before noon
- 12 am – at midnight
- 4 pm – at tea time

2 👥 Can the students describe what is happening in the picture? Are there any unusual things? By describing the actions using the present continuous, they will have an easier task converting sentences to the past continuous later.

3 It is important to make this a dramatic moment. Once the students have called out lots of lovely present continuous sentences, you can stop and say:
Okay, cover the picture ... But wait, these people are not here right now. Look, it is dark outside. This is clearly not 'now'. In fact, this picture was taken YESTERDAY (point over your shoulder) *at 3 pm. Can you tell me, what the people WERE doing yesterday at 3 pm?*
You may need to prompt them in case the past continuous is completely new to them or if they are a bit shy: *What was the baker doing? What were... ?* etc.
This is the time for accuracy. Students really should get the target structure correct.

T The baker was delivering a wedding cake.
F Two children were *taking a cat for a walk / walking a cat on a lead.*
F A *woman* was cleaning some windows.
F A woman was pushing *a dog* in a pram.
T A man was looking at his watch.
F Four women were *doing yoga* on the pavement.
F A busker was *singing opera.*

4
Simple revision allowing for greater student talking time. Make sure you move around and monitor. Direct students who are still struggling with the structure to the grammar box.

5
1.14 Students listen to a conversation in which three people talk about where they were and what they were doing when the Berlin wall came down. Have them look at the three gapped sentences in the diagram before they listen.

Martin was lying in bed …
George was having dinner with his girlfriend on the Ku'damm …
Marta and her boyfriend were shopping near Union Square …

6
As a lead-in to this sorting exercise, which focuses on things people say when reacting to news or listening to stories, you can have students listen to the conversation on track 14 again and note the interjections they hear. (*You're joking! Cool. Really?*)

You're surprised. Wow! Really? No way! You're joking!
You like what you hear. That sounds great! Cool! Good idea!
You feel sorry for the other person. Better luck next time. Oh dear.
You understand. OK. Right. I see.

7
Encourage your students to be as creative as possible with completing these sentences. Having fun with the language is a good sign that someone is making progress.

Before students make their own sentences with simple past and past continuous, you can use **photocopiable 6** to give your students some extra practice with the sentence structure.

- Cut out all the cards and hand them out, one per person. (You can make extra copies of some cards if you need more.)
- Tell students that they must not show their card to anybody.
- Students mill around and read their sentence halves to each other until they find a match, at which point they can stop looking and sit down.
- Once everybody is seated, students can read out their sentences for the whole class.

Unit 3 Part B

8 You can set this exercise up as pairwork or group work so students have to say the dates out loud. Go around and monitor their progress.

🔑 1 F   2 C   3 G   4 E   5 A   6 D   7 B

9 👥 People generally like talking about what they were doing when some major event happened. Let the students discuss this freely, without worrying too much about accuracy.

C You'll never believe this! coursebook pages 30–31

1 A nice little quiz to get people thinking of Ireland. It is likely some of your students will have been and will know the answers though they may get the answer to number 1 wrong!

🔑
1 False. The Czechs drink the most beer (157 litres per person per year!), Ireland is second and Germany third.
2 True
3 True
4 False. They use the euro.

2 A comparatively long reading. Encourage your students to keep reading, even if they don't understand every word.

🔑 He did it to win a one-hundred-pound bet (and as an excuse to write a funny book, which they are now turning into a film. See www.tonyhawks.com for more information.)

3 Encourage your students to work together on this True/False exercise.

🔑
1 **T**
2 **F** The man was holding out his *arm*.
3 **F** When they saw the man, Kieran *just drove by/kept driving*.
4 **F** *Ten* years later Tony was staying at a *bed and breakfast with friends*.
5 **F** While he and his friends *were drinking wine one evening*, he told them about the hitchhiker.
6 **T**

4 This is the first of two exercises dealing with this unit's **key verb look**. If students have trouble matching the sentence parts, have them study the box first.

🔑 1 B   2 C   3 E   4 A   5 F   6 D

5 **Key verb: look.** Your students may not be particularly creative and will just write down the first thing they think of. Encourage them to come up with some more ideas.

> **Extra activity:** Get your students to take it in turns to act out expressions with *look*, while the other students guess what they're doing.

6 A nice collocation exercise. You might want to have students work together or even turn it into a competition to see which group or pair finds the most collocations in a minute.

be home, a friend, on holiday, happy
call the police, a friend
get home, dressed
go home, on holiday, for a swim, to bed
have a friend, a chat with a friend, a bath, an accident, lunch
make coffee, a cake
look for a nice hotel, happy

7 This is a longer reading activity and a comparatively quiet phase of the lesson, giving you the opportunity to give extra help to those who need it.

A few years ago **I was staying** at my friend George's cattle ranch in Texas for the summer. One day we **drove** to Dallas for the afternoon. We **didn't come** back until late in the evening. **I was** very tired and **went** straight to bed. While I **was lying** there still awake, I suddenly **heard** a very loud splash. **I rushed** out to George's swimming pool at the back of the house. I **couldn't believe** my eyes. There **was** a big hole in the fence and a huge brown cow **was standing** in the middle of the pool …

… Well, I was quite surprised! I **screamed** at the top of my voice but the cow in the swimming pool just **looked** scared and **didn't move**. While I **was screaming**, George **rushed** out and **jumped** into the pool. He **tried** to get the cow out, but it **was** impossible. George finally **called** the cops. While they **were getting** the cow out of the pool, I **went** back to my room to look for a camera. But when I **returned**, the cow was already back in the field. What a relief!

8 Try to get your students to be creative with this writing exercise. You can join in with the questions when you are listening to stories.

9 **And finally …** An exercise to review and consolidate some of the structures the students studied in the unit. It can be done for homework if time is short.

> **Extension activity:** Students can write sentences for you to change so that they are true for you. Feel free to lie if some questions are too personal!

Unit 3 Part C

4

 At the end of unit 4 your students should:
- be able to talk about their likes and dislikes in a variety of ways and use expressions that take the gerund.
- have practised a range of comparatives and superlatives.
- be able to talk about work (both inside and outside the home) and the qualities needed for various jobs.
- have practised using modal verbs such as *have to* and *mustn't*.
- have learnt various ways to talk about pros and cons.

A A change of scenery   coursebook pages 34–35

1 Students discuss what they can do with the four tools shown in the photos. With the students working in pairs or groups, you can listen in on their conversations.

> Possible answers (there are no doubt millions more):
>
> | | |
> |---|---|
> | scissors | I can cut paper, string, hair. |
> | bucket & squeegee | I can clean my car, my windows, the shower, my mirrors. |
> | spade | I can dig my garden or a well. |
> | feather duster | I can clean (or dust) my shelves and furniture. I can get rid of spiders' webs. |

2 Match up the collocations – some nice humour here with the wrong answers. You may like to pre-teach *to weed*, *to dust* and *to feed*. Encourage your students to work together to match up the collocations.

> | | | |
> |---|---|---|
> | water the plants | cut the grass | iron the clothes |
> | weed the garden | feed the baby, pets | vacuum the car, flat |
> | wash the car | clean the car, flat, windows | dust the furniture |

3 A nice exercise to get the students to recycle the collocations that they have just looked at. Encourage your students to discuss this in pairs or small groups.

4 **1.17** Students listen to someone talking about working as a house-sitter in Australia. Can your students hear some Australian English? (Answer: *down under, G'day, barbie*)

> Helena loves Australia (down under) and chatting with Australians.
> Helena hates dusting and the sand (which gets everywhere).
> Helena has no strong feelings about the heat.
> Helena is looking forward to seeing her mum and dad.

5 A simple matching exercise, practising expressions that take the gerund. You may need to play track 17 again for students to check their answers.

1 She enjoys — meeting people and learning Australian English.
2 She can't stand — vacuuming and dusting.
3 She is looking forward to — spending the holiday with her parents.
4 She doesn't mind — living in a hot climate.
5 She is afraid of — breaking an expensive antique.

6 Students have the opportunity to discuss their own likes and dislikes – hopefully using the expressions + gerund that they have been looking at. The grammar box at the bottom of the page will help them.

7 A reading exercise based on the same topic the students have been discussing. They can discuss with their partner whether house-sitting is for them, or not. Your students may need help with the pronunciation of *comfortable*. Many native speakers don't pronounce the 'or' in the middle and it is definitely not stressed as many foreign speakers tend to say it.

8 A sorting exercise to make students aware of the variety of ways in which we make comparatives in English. There is *some* logic to this system. Adjectives of one syllable tend to have *-er* in the comparative form. If the adjective with one syllable ends with a consonant, vowel, consonant, and doesn't end in *x* or *y*, then the consonant is doubled. With adjectives ending in *y*, the *y* is replaced by *-ier*. Adjectives with two or more syllables tend to take *more* or *less*. Sadly, the irregular ones will just have to be learnt.

older	hotter	busier	more famous	worse
cheaper	bigger	roomier	less expensive	better
nicer	slimmer		less lonely	
			more fun	
			more luxurious	
			more comfortable	

9 A quick reading exercise and then a discussion of the best place to house-sit. Listen in on your students' conversations and help them where necessary.

10 A final opportunity for students to talk about their preferences. Encourage them to justify their choices. Hopefully they will use many comparative forms in their discussion but don't force them to use the structure.

B Let's get down to work

coursebook pages 36–37

1 A fun warm-up activity to give the lesson a lively start.

> Use **photocopiable 7** to hand out the job titles to your students. If you have a large board, you can divide the class into two teams. If you have a smaller board, you can have one student drawing the job on the board and both teams guessing the job. If you have no board, your students could mime the jobs.

2 A reading exercise about three very different jobs. You may like to pre-teach: *Barista, varying, to lose one's head.* Students can then discuss which job they would like to do.

1 Job 3   5 Job 3
2 Job 1   6 Job 3
3 Job 2   7 Job 1
4 Jobs 2 & 3

3 An opportunity for your students to practise using modal verbs. Note that German native speakers often confuse *mustn't* and *don't have to*.

1 don't have to, don't have to, mustn't
2 must, don't have to
3 mustn't, need to

4 More practice on modals.

Suggested answers:

You have to	arrive on time, be friendly and polite.
You can	make yourself lunch with food from the fridge, speak English, work with your own equipment, help yourself to water and coffee, make local phone calls, wear a uniform.
You mustn't	wear shoes, invite your friends over to watch TV.

5 A fun activity for your students to do in small groups. You may like to model the exercise before they go into groups by choosing a new job for yourself. Encourage the students to use some of the phrases in the box on the right. Hopefully, they will also be using the correct modal structures.

6 **1.18** A nice review of superlatives, which students will most likely have encountered in previous courses. The students hear Mike talking to a job counsellor. Note that not all the items in Box A have a corresponding item in Box B.

🔑
My biggest	challenge
My most boring	-
The busiest	-
The easiest	thing for me to do
The best	job in the world
The worst	thing for me is routine
The most secure	job out there
The most important	thing for me right now
Your most difficult	-
Your highest	priorities

👥 Students then play job counsellor and suggest a job for Mike. Have the class vote on the best ideas.

> **Additional exercise:** If you feel your students need more than a review of superlatives, you may like to give some practical examples by asking some questions: *Is the Rhine short or long? (Long!) And what about the Mississippi River, is that shorter than the Rhine? (No! It's longer!) Oh, but the Nile is very short, isn't it? (No, it's the longest river in the world!)*
> You could do the same with three tall students in your class and elicit the adjective, comparative and superlative from your students.

7 In this exercise there is room for the students to be imaginative with their use of superlatives.

🔑 Suggested answers:

1 most/least dangerous, most/least exciting, most/least rewarding, etc.
2 most/least exciting, liveliest/most boring, dirtiest, safest, most popular, most expensive/cheapest, etc.
3 best/worst, most/least exciting, easiest/most difficult, etc.
4 most/least interesting, hottest/coldest, most/least pleasant, most/least popular, etc.

8 👥 **And finally ...** Students work in pairs to talk about their town. If you yourself are new to the area, you could use this exercise to get some genuine information. If some of your students are new to the area, get them to ask their fellow students for help. Clearly there's no right or wrong answers and your students will enjoy discussing their own personal preferences.

C All in a day's work!

coursebook pages 38–39

1 A brainstorming activity (which could also be done alone) for students to think of a wide variety of jobs.

2 A reading exercise about three very different jobs. You may like to pre-teach: *fancy dress, thick-skinned, rotten, sensible, varying, to lose one's head*. Make sure the students only read one job profile. You could divide your class into three groups: A, B and C. The As read job profile 1, The Bs, job profile 2 and the Cs, job profile 3. Once they have read the text, you match them up with other groups, so an A, a B and a C sit together and tell the others about the skills required for their job and what job they think it might be.

    🔑 1 Singing telegram
         2 Pet detective
         3 Walking advertisement

Note that students can combine words in the blue box to make eight different job titles, three of which are the jobs profiled here. You can let students do this part of the exercise on their own as needed, or you might want to have weaker students do the exercise before they start reading the profiles.

    🔑
lead singer	zookeeper
pet detective	dog walker
newspaper seller	singing telegram
walking advertisement	street sweeper

3 A chance for your students to practise using modal verbs.

    🔑 Model answer for job 1:
         I have to be friendly with my clients – even when they don't like me.
         I don't need to study for years to do my job.
         I mustn't be late for my appointments.
         I don't mind working late at night or early morning. The tips are often better!
         I enjoy bringing a bit of happiness into people's lives.

4 👥 Your students get the opportunity to read out the statements they wrote in exercise 3 and listen to those of their neighbours. They can then debate the merits of the various jobs, hopefully while using the comparative and superlative form of the adjectives given.

5 A look at this unit's **key verb work** with an exercise that involves personalization. (No answer key as answers will vary by student.)

> Use **photocopiable 8** to get your students to discuss people's jobs and the equipment they use to do them.
>
> - Make enough copies so that each group of 3-5 students has a full set of cards. Cut out the cards and distribute them, making sure each student in the group gets a mix of A, B and C cards.
> - Each group works then together to find 'full sets' of A, B and C cards. Students take turn reading out their A cards and then working together to make logical sentences by finding the corresponding B and C cards.
> - At the end of the activity, you can review some of the new vocabulary that cropped up. For example, ask students who else uses a hose (e.g. a gardener), a ladder, a broom, a stethoscope, etc.

6 **1.19** In this listening comprehension exercise, your students will hear different people talking about their jobs.

    1 C   2 E   3 D   4 B   5 F   6 A

Before they listen again to recreate the extracts, get them to read the texts and try to decide whether the statements are positive or negative. How much do they remember from the previous listening(s)?

    A There's one big drawback, more challenging, have to run
    B The brilliant thing is, better informed
    C Unfortunately, dumber, louder
    D It's the best job, dressing up, meeting
    E The worst part is, all types of weather, pets
    F Well, I'm afraid, giving

7 In this exercise there is room for the students to practise the language they have just been looking at (comparatives, superlatives, expressing pros and cons, etc.) in a new way. Get them to work in pairs (or small groups) and monitor their conversations.

Journal 1

See notes in the teaching tips (page 10) on ways to use the material in the journals.

Coursebook pages 42–49

Six adjectives to describe travelers

Before reading
- Your students get into groups and brainstorm lots of qualities they think a good traveller should have. They write down a list and exchange the list with another group. Were there any qualities in common? Any surprises? (You might want to point out that Lisa Lubin uses American spelling conventions, e. g. *travelers instead of travellers*.)

After reading
- **What about you?** In pairs, the students go through Lisa's six adjectives and discuss whether they possess those qualities or not. They can also discuss whether they think Lisa got it right. Are there other qualities which are more important for a good traveller?
- **Six adjectives:** Lisa wrote about six adjectives to describe travelers. Get your students to think of another group of people (writers? politicians? TV personalities?) and get them to write down six adjectives to describe them. In the feedback session they can read the adjectives out and the other students have to guess what group is being described.

Fun in the sun!

Before reading
- The students look at the photos and discuss which people they would enjoy having a drink with. (Or perhaps which ones they could survive having a drink with!)

After reading
- Get the students to talk about Benidorm in the 1950s compared to today.
- The students discuss things they (now) know about Derren Litten, the writer of Benidorm. Would they like to meet him?

The world according to …

Before reading
- In 2002, international tourists made 665 million trips. But that means that about 6 billion people didn't make an international trip. Get your students to think where most international travellers come from in the world. They might find this easier to do by continent rather than country by country. Then they can look at the world map. Were their ideas correct?

After reading
- **Facts and figures:** Get the students to look at three other world maps. Can they explain the reasons behind some of the figures? Why is cinema attendance so high in India? Why are there so few international tourists from South America?
- **More world maps:** What other data would the students like to see represented in this format? (There are over 700 different ones.) Those students with an internet connection may like to check out the worldmapper website and see what else is available. Can they report back for the other students?

City break: Chicago
Before reading
- Get your students to discuss what they know about Chicago and what they would like to know about Chicago. While they are reading they can check to confirm their ideas, or, hopefully, get the answers to some of their questions.

After reading
- **But we've got ... :** Chicago has many interesting features. How do they compare with where the students live. Have them compare the two places, e. g.: *Chicago has got world class museums but we've got a brilliant technical museum. In Chicago you can eat a Chicago Hot Dog but here we can eat a fantastic doner kebab.*
- **New words:** Get the students to write down some of the words that they haven't seen before. Then get them to divide the words into two groups: *words that I think I understand and words that I haven't got a clue about.* Encourage them to look at the word in context and often the meaning will become clear to them. More importantly, there may have been a few words that they didn't understand, but encourage them to look on the bright side; they did understand – or were able to work out – 95 % of the words, which was enough to understand the text.
- **I'd like to ...:** Get them to discuss what they would like to do in Chicago. Then they can exchange ideas with others in the group.

Alien convention
Before reading
- Ask your students: Are there aliens 'out there' which sometimes visit us? and What do they think of people who believe there are aliens 'out there' which sometimes visit us?

After reading
- **Role-play:** If your students enjoy role-plays, you could role-play a hotel scene between Ellen and some of the alien visitors. This could either be done face-to-face or on the telephone. Give the aliens some time to come up with some ideas about where they have come from and whether they have any special requests.

5

At the end of unit 5 your students should:
- have discussed a wide variety of food items.
- have practised how to use *some* and *any* correctly.
- have practised countable and uncountable nouns.
- know when to use *how much* and *how many*.
- have practised short answers and reviewed the tenses.
- have practised making recommendations.
- have built up a healthy appetite!

A That's tasty! coursebook pages 50–51

1 A nice warmer to get your students thinking about food. Let's hope they had something to eat before coming to class! In case you're wondering, an okra is a bit like a small courgette.

meat/seafood:	mussels, ostrich, quail	
vegetables:	artichoke, okra, yam	
fruit:	gooseberry, kiwi, pineapple	

Get your students to think of more unusual foods and, in small groups, write down a list. When they read out five items from the list, can the others decide which category they belong to?

2 Still with the theme of food but also giving your students some practice of *some* and *any*. There are some cases in which both forms can be used: *Have you got any Peruvian coffee?/ Have you got some Peruvian coffee?* In the second case the speaker is more confident that the coffee seller has some Peruvian coffee.

1 someone/anyone 4 some, any
2 any 5 something
3 something, any 6 some

In the second part of the exercise, the students match the three answers with the questions above, and then write three more answers for the other questions.

A 3   B 1   C 2

Suggested answers:
4 Yes, there's some English wine over there.
5 Sweets? I saw someone selling popcornsicles.
6 Yes please! I love exotic fruit.

Unit 5 Part A

3 Students read an excerpt form a brochure about an annual food festival in Chicago. They then do exercise 4.

4 👥 A simple comprehension exercise based on the reading text above. Students can then work in pairs to write more questions and answers.

🗝 1 It takes place around the Fourth of July in Grant Park in Chicago.
   2 More than 3 million.
   3 Over 70.

> 📄 **Photocopiable 9** will give your students practice discussing food items.
>
> - Make a copy and cut up the cards. Put them in three piles: A, B and C.
> - Mix up the cards in each pile and leave them face down.
> - You might want to pre-teach: *a rasher of bacon* (a slice of bacon), *gravy* (a meaty sauce), *custard* (vanilla sauce), *trifle*, *cinnamon*, *minced beef* and *gruyere*.
> - Invite three students to the front of the class. Explain that they have just had a very special meal. Then ask them to tell the group what they had.
> - The first student reads out one piece from pile A, then the second student reads out a piece from pile B and finally the third student reads out a piece from pile C.
> - Once the 'meal' has been read out, the other students call out either: *That's delicious!* or *That's disgusting!*

5 A quick exercise to give your students some practice of *much* and *many*.

🗝 1 much   4 much
   2 much   5 many
   3 many

6 In the first part of this exercise, the students can discuss what they think the various booths will sell. (Note that these are all actual booths at the festival, and can be found on the map.)

1.21 They then listen to a recording and can see how accurate their guesses were.

🗝 Abbey Pub (9)   Irish Guinness, tasty Irish specialities
   Vienna Beef/Gold Coast   Chicago style hot dogs with pickles, hot peppers,
   Dogs (27)   tomatoes, mustard (and a dry bun)
   Arya Bhavan (51)   Samosas
   Garrett Popcorn Shops (52)   A popcornsicle*

*A popsicle is a kind of ice lolly (see photo on page 50)

In the final part of the exercise, the students have to match up the food items with the descriptions that were used to describe them in the recording.

⚟ 1 D 2 F, H 3 G, C 4 A 5 B, E

7 👥 The lesson ends with a fun game in which students describe their favourite foods to their partner who have to guess what food is being described.

B Naughty but nice! coursebook pages 52–53

(The title comes from an advertising campaign in England for cream cakes – which people knew were not healthy, but very tasty.)

1 👥 A nice 'find someone who' warmer to get your students talking. You may need to pre-teach: *to eat out* and *to skip a meal*.

2 👥 The students ask each other about holidays and special days that they celebrate and the food and drink they consume then.

3 At this stage, the students are just guessing what is happening in the pictures.

⚟ Suggested answers:

1 The man appears to be working at an auction. It looks like he's selling some food.
2 The people seem to be licking the cars.
3 The people are picking something from the trees. Are they long beans?

4 The students read the text 'Sweet treats'. In this part of the exercise they just have to answer two questions. Note that the British English word for *candy* is *sweets*.

⚟ 1 The text goes with picture 2.
2 Sweetest Day is on the 3rd Saturday in October so you (or your students) can calculate how many days until the next one.

5 👥 Some practice for your students at forming questions (and answering them). If they're having problems, they can have a look at the blue box below the exercise.

⚟ 1 Did, work   5 Did, make
2 Was   6 Are, licking
3 Did, give   7 Do, think, is
4 Do, celebrate

Unit 5 Part B

When your students come to answer the questions, encourage them to use short answers, but not to repeat long parts of the question. *Have you ever been to the carnival in Rio and danced all night long? No, I have never been to the carnival in Rio and danced all night long* is a common error among students who want to be 'correct'. A native speaker would never say that. They would answer: *Yes, I have. It was brilliant!* Or perhaps: *No, I haven't. I'm not a big fan of dancing.*

Suggested answers:

1 Yes, he did. Somewhere near the Great Lakes.
2 No, he wasn't. He had enough money to buy sweets for the local people.
3 No, he didn't. He gave away sweets and chocolate.
4 No, they don't. It is only popular in some parts of the US.
5 No, they didn't. They covered some cars in chocolate.
6 No, they aren't. They're licking cars.
7 (The students must decide for themselves)

6 This little section allows students to discuss similar 'special days' that they celebrate in their region. This can be very enlightening teachers who are not from the area. Get them to discuss in groups before a larger feedback session.

> **Photocopiable 10** will allow your students to discuss food, drink and activities within the humorous concept of a new special day.
>
> - Make a copy and cut out the six cards. (There are eight per sheet.)
> - Ask your students to remind you of the various 'special days' that they know about.
> - Explain that the government wants to introduce a new special day – and that they have asked you to get some ideas. (You may have to wink if some students think you are telling the truth.)
> - Explain that they have 10 (or 15) minutes as a group to come up with the ideas for the new special day with help from information on the sheet. They should make notes.
> - Each group then stands up and presents their ideas to the class. Which ideas does the class think should be adopted?

7 A nice follow-up exercise in which the students get the details behind pictures 1 and 3. Lots of practice of forming questions and giving short answers.

8 **1.22** Listening comprehension about a scene in a restaurant. Nothing too difficult here though you may have to play the recording more than once.

1 Do you have any preferences?
2 How about something spicy?
3 Do you prefer white or red?

9 An exercise – which could become reality! In small groups, the students discuss where they might like to have a meal together. There are some useful questions and comments on the right. Perhaps you could join the group with the best suggestion!

C Keep it simple   coursebook pages 54–55

1 Your students have to match up some national specialities with where they come from. They should be happy if they know five out of eight.

sashimi – Japan   haggis – Scotland
poutine – Canada (Quebec) paella – Spain
pasta – Italy   hot dogs – America
curry – India   borscht – Ukraine*

*although popular among many East European countries

2 A quick reading exercise about Sam Zien's cooking classes. The students then tick which statements they think are true about Sam. You may like to explain the word *fancy* in the phrase *fancy ingredients*. Don't expect your students to get the answers until they have read the passage in exercise 3.

1 ✓
2 ✓
3 ✗ There are no fancy ingredients.
4 ✓
5 ✓ (his dogs)
6 ✗ They film his show in his home.

3 The students read the passage to check their answers in exercise 2. Encourage them to read it through without a dictionary – you can always help them afterwards. The students then create questions which give the answers that are given.

Suggested answers (or rather questions):

1 Do they film Sam in his own home?
2 Are there a lot of ingredients in Sam's recipes?
3 Did Sam have any experience of television when he began?
4 Did the industry experts help him?

Encourage the students to ask more questions about Sam's (and their partner's) cooking talents.

4 👥 A fun exercise in which your students try to plan a meal. They first note down what they have in their fridges, then plan a meal.

👥 Once it is planned, they should try to encourage other people to try their dish. Allow them to move around the room and discuss their 'menu' with as many people as possible. In the feedback session, find out which pair produced the most interesting/popular/unusual food.

5 Key verb: try. You should give your students some more practice of the key verb once they have done the exercise – or tried to do it!

🔑 1 C   2 F   3 D   4 A   5 E   6 B

6 🎧 1.23 Your students should make recommendations for Zoe and Keith. Make sure they notice their preferences and allergies. They might not know what sambousek is but it is explained in the listening exercise. They then listen to hear what was ordered.

🔑 For Zoe   the mixed salad with an Italian dressing
   For Keith   spicy beef sambousek

7 A fun quiz to test your students' attitude to food. This could lead into a discussion of how food habits are changing. The students also have to decide whether the questions begin with *How much* or *How many*.

🔑 1 How many   1 How much
    2 How many   2 How many

👥 In the final part, the students turn to page 130 to get their results and find out if they are 'food dinosaurs', 'apprentice chefs' or 'master chefs'. The instructions at the end of the results are meant to be humourous, but the students can mingle after the questionnaire and find out how their fellow students did.

6

At the end of unit 6 your students should:
- have practised present continuous with future meaning.
- have practised invitations and making arrangements.
- have talked about a variety of leisure activities.
- be able to use *going to*-future.
- have a wider range of adverbs.
- have discussed ways to reduce stress.
- have listened to a range of people talking about the future.
- have studied the key verb *to take*.

A What's up? coursebook pages 58–59

1 A nice warmer to get your students thinking about leisure activities. In the feedback session, ask your students about interesting similarities and differences in their ranking.

2 Reading comprehension. The students read an email from Zoe and try to work out which kind of event she and her friends are going to visit. There are enough clues in the email for them to work it out.

⚬── She's going to a sand sculpture festival.

3 This exercise introduces a structure known as the 'diary future', when we use the present continuous to talk about events in the future, typically for the kinds of things that you would write in your diary. A nice way to introduce this to invite one of your students out for a drink.

Teacher:	Dirk, would you like to have a drink with me tomorrow?
Dirk:	That sounds good!
Teacher:	What time is good for you, Dirk?
Dirk:	About eight o'clock?
Teacher:	(Looking at diary) Oh, I'm sorry, Dirk. **I'm having** dinner with Andreas at eight o'clock.

Then get your students think about the tense that you used (the present continuous) and the time period it refers to in the example (tomorrow at eight o'clock).

⚬── 1 False. They're going to a sand sculpture festival.

2 False. Jamie's coming later and Holly isn't coming at all.

3 True

4 True

5 False. Hers isn't working.

6 Not sure.

Unit 6 Part A

4 **1.25** More practice of the diary future based on a listening comprehension. Note that there is also an example of the timetable future, where we use the present simple for a future event that appears on a timetable. In this example it is: *The performance begins at …* Another example (not from the book): *Hurry up, the train leaves in ten minutes!*

	Who?	What?	When?
1	Jamie is calling Fred	A thriller at the theatre	Friday at 8 pm
2	Sara is calling Fred	A barbeque	Friday at about 3 pm

1.26 Students listen again to see what Fred has decided to do. You may like to debate whether the students think Fred is telling the truth – or perhaps he thinks Jamie is boring and prefers Sara's company!

Fred is going shopping and then he's going to the barbeque with Katy.

5 Students practise making arrangements. They can either use (or make) their own diaries or you can use the photocopiable below.

> **Photocopiable 11** will give your students practice of the diary future.
>
> - Make enough copies so that each student has a diary.
> - Explain to the students that you are going to make their social lives (even more) exciting. Tell them that you have copies of their personal diaries and that you will hand them out. Their task is to fill their diary with some interesting activities – either suggested by their colleagues, or their own ideas.
> - It's a good idea to model the dialogue before you begin.
>   Teacher: *Hey Michael, would you like to play ping pong with me on Friday evening?*
>   Michael: *Sorry, I'm having a drink with Claudia Schiffer on Friday. OR: Yes, that sounds great! I'm a ping pong champion! What time do you want to play?* (Not *What time are we playing?* as the activity has not been finalized.)
> - Give the students five minutes to ask as many people to join in their various activities.
> - Follow up: Ask some students about their arrangements: *What are you doing on Wednesday?*

6 The lesson ends with a fun game of tic-tac-toe (or 'noughts and crosses' in Britain). The students should play with their partner and can only 'win' one square at a time.

B Take it easy!

coursebook pages 60–61

1 Your students discuss the leisure activities associated with the four elements. Here are some suggested answers:

Earth	Air	Fire	Water
gardening	kite flying	fire juggling	swimming
pottery	gliding	fire walking	sailing
	model aeroplanes	barbeque	fishing

2 The students look for clues in the illustration to identify which people are going to do various things. They can use the structures in the switchboard to do this.

Suggested answers:

1 I think the woman in high heels is going to meet somebody for the first time (because she's refreshing/checking her make-up.)

2 I think the woman with the newspaper is going to work all weekend. She looks like she's a workaholic.

3 I think the couple with the dogs are going to go for a walk through the woods.

3 **1.27** Students then listen to check their answers (see correct answers above) and will hear a lot of other examples with the *going to*-future.

1 It's going to be very stressful.

2 It's not going to be easy though.

3 It's going to be so romantic.

4 Speaking exercise. Make sure you monitor while your students are speaking and join in the conversation, keeping it as natural as possible.

5 A quick exercise to get your students to think about ways to relax. It is nice to get them to work together to produce a list.

6 A reading exercise about stress and ways to reduce it. Ask your students to discuss which of the three methods they would like to try. You could also have them underline the adverbs in anticipation of exercises 7 and 8. There are seven: *extremely, seriously, especially, heartily, hard, carefully* and *definitely*.

7 A quick exercise with adverbs. Encourage your students to put the verb and adverb into a natural sentence to 'hear' if they fit together

⚊○ Suggested answers:

speak	well, quickly, fast, loudly, carefully
walk	quickly, fast
drive	well, badly, quickly, fast, carefully
dance	well, badly, quickly, crazily
work	well, badly, hard, quickly, fast, carefully
eat	well, quickly, fast

8 Students fill the gaps with adjectives and adverbs, then ask each other the questions.

⚊○ Suggested answers:
1 well/badly
2 interesting/fun
3 relaxing, good
4 fast/quickly
5 carefully

C   Let's take a break

coursebook pages 62–63

1 An exercise to get your students thinking about the future. Encourage them to debate the statements, and ask questions.

2 A simple matching exercise of the interesting texts and the photos. You may want to pre-teach: *butterflies, haunted* and *poo!*

⚊○ 1 C   2 D   3 E   4 B   5 A

In the second part of the exercise the students have to look for vocabulary within the texts. Encourage them to help each other.

⚊○ 1 admission
2 to have butterflies in your stomach
3 banquet
4 cutlery
5 disgusting
6 a tongue-twister

3 👥 The students plan a holiday together – it is a good idea that they make a few notes. Once they have planned it, then can tell another pair about their plans. Now that the plans have been made, they should use *going to*-future to describe them. You may need to model the structure before they begin.

4 👥 A nice recycling exercise in which the students write a short email to a friend. Students may ask about *atb* at the end of the email – it is an abbreviation for *all the best*, a nice way to end your emails for friends or very good colleagues.

5 `1.28` A listening comprehension. The students will hear Vera talking about her weekend.

🔑   1 explore the area
    2 take part in a medieval banquet
    3 celebrate a special occasion with champagne
    4 take a train
    5 take part in a workshop

George repeats the words because he is either surprised, or he wants further clarification.

6 `1.29` Sounds good. A simple exercise in which students have to work out what words the people will use to make it sound natural. Remind the students to look at how George repeated some of Vera's words.

🔑   1 Next weekend?
    2 Rhyl?
    3 Too far?

7 👥 A short writing exercise based on Vera's weekend. You might want to check that they know how to turn the adjectives into adverbs before they start.

🔑   1 well   5 wet
    2 dry   6 delicious
    3 badly   7 quickly
    4 fantastic

8 Key verb: take. The students modify the sentences so that they are true for them.

9 👥 **How long does it take?** A nice exercise in which your students ask each other questions about how long things take. They can use the phrases in the box but they can also make up their own questions.

> 📄 Use **photocopiable 12** to help revise the vocabulary in unit 6.
>
> - Make copies so that there are enough for one between two students.
> - Show students the crossword format and explain that all the words appear in unit 6. You might need to explain *across* and *down*.
> - Encourage students to talk together to solve the clues. If you have a competitive class, you could also turn it into a race to see which pair can finish first.
>
>   🔑 Across: 2 jazz, 7 emigrate, 8 spa, 10 circus, 11 picnic, 15 quickly, 16 massage.
>   Down: 1 camcorder, 3 laugh, 4 gardening, 5 cactus, 6 rabbit, 9 titbits, 12 cinema, 13 relax 14 kite

7

> **At the end of unit 7 your students should:**
> - be able use the present perfect correctly.
> - be able to use the present perfect or simple past at the correct time.
> - have practised already and not ... yet.
> - be able to make and receive phone calls.
> - be able to take messages from phone calls.
> - have written short promotional texts.

A Been there, seen that!   coursebook pages 66–67

1 A nice twist on a simple exercise – the students match up well known tourist destinations with the flags of the countries in which they are found.

>   1 The Grand Canyon   4 The Great Wall of China
>   2 The Coliseum   5 The Taj Mahal
>   3 Sugar Loaf Mountain   6 Loch Ness

After the exercise, your students discuss which places they would like to visit and why.

> **Extension activity:** Get students to draw pictures of famous places they have been. They then show them to the group and they have to decide where the student has been. It is a good idea for you to draw a really bad drawing of a famous monument (such as the Eiffel Tower) so that students whose drawing skills are not great will not feel embarrassed.

2 A reading exercise about Murphy the gnome. (Make sure students don't pronounce the g.) Encourage your students to read the passage without using a dictionary (or asking you). They don't need to understand every word.

>   1 has been
>   2 has stood in a shark's mouth
>   3 has climbed a mountain
>   4 has ridden a motorbike
>   5 has written a book
>   6 This answer will depend on the students' own experience.

3 Get your students to fill in the table showing the infinitive (*to be, to go* etc) and the past participle (*I have* **been**, *She has* **had** etc.).

56   Unit 7 Part A

1 been	5 stood	9 live
2 do	6 ridden	10 visited
3 have	7 taken	
4 swum*	8 write	

*though we also use *been swimming* if we are just talking about the activity.

> **Extension activity:** Once the students have filled in the table, it is important that they use the information in it! Get them to ask each other lots of questions about where they have been, how many times they've ridden a horse etc.

> Use **photocopiable 13** to give your students more practice with the present perfect.
>
> - Cut out the cards and hand them out, one per person.
> - Explain that this is a speaking exercise, so the students mustn't look at each other's cards.
> - Students mill around and read their sentence halves to each other until they find a match. (Both people should read their part; even if they don't match, the object is to practise their English, not just match up the sentences.)
> - Once the students find their match, they can sit down (or take new cards – if there are some extras – and do another round).
> - During the feedback session, you can have some pairs read out their complete sentences.
>
> There's a lot of humour here so the students will see it as an enjoyable exercise rather than a boring grammar exercise.

4 A nice exercise to get your students to use the target structure (the present perfect) in a natural way. Get them to work in pairs to decide who they are going to ask. Check that they know the correct structure by letting a couple of people model their questions before everyone starts talking. It will be anarchy, but hopefully they will be using the target structure to ask (and answer) a lot of questions.

5 The students look at the illustrations and should be able to work out where Davina has been and what she did in those places. Here are some suggested answers as there is room for debate.

1 She's been to New York. I think she visited the Statue of Liberty.
2 She's been to Egypt. I think she went diving in the Red Sea
3 She's been to London. I think she went to St. Paul's Cathedral.
4 She's been to South Africa. I think she went on a safari.
5 She's been to the Grand Canyon. I think she took a helicopter trip there.

6 **2.2** Davina (the woman from exercise 5) and Ian (a man she meets at a party) talk about their travels. Before they listen, can your students unscramble the sentences? Then when they hear the recording, the should be able to hear who says what.

🔑

	Ian	Davina
1 I haven't been to Siberia but I've been to South Africa twice.	✗	✓
2 Have you ever seen the pyramids?	✗	✓
3 I've never flown further south than Majorca.	✓	✗
4 I've been to the States several times.	✗	✓
5 I've never even been on the London Eye.	✓	✗

7 **And finally …** A very natural set of questions and answers which the students have to match up.

🔑   1 D   2 A   3 B   4 C   5 E

Get your students to ask each other these questions (and any others they would like to ask). In the feedback session, you don't need to get every answer from every student: just ask a few for their most interesting answers.

B You've actually done that?
coursebook pages 68–69

1 A nice warmer with a very useful structure: *Have you ever…?* Students match up the two parts and make a question with *Have you ever…?* There are many possible questions. Here are some of them:

🔑
1 Have you ever driven	a Porsche? (note we ride motorbikes, not drive them).
2 Have you ever won	a prize/a Porsche/a motorbike/a race?
3 Have you ever sung	on TV/karaoke/at a wedding?
4 Have you ever made	sushi/a birthday cake?
5 Have you ever been	on TV/at a wedding?

2 A nice way to get the whole class talking. Using two 'to do' lists as a launch pad, the students ask each other about the various things on the list. You may want to make sure your students can create the questions properly before they start the exercise. In the feedback session, just ask a few people for the most interesting things they found out. Don't forget, you will probably switch to the simple past to discuss the event itself: *"Klaus has read 'War and Peace' this year." "Really, Klaus? Did you enjoy it?" "No, it was boring."*

3 **2.3** Your students first look at the picture to decide whether they think Mike and Mary have done the various things. Then there is a listening comprehension to find out more.

Unit 7 Part B

🗝 Mike has found a new job.   Mary has started playing the guitar again.
He has started learning Spanish.   She has started volunteering at a soup kitchen.
He has bought a new laptop.

4 An exercise to practise *already, yet*, and *not yet*. Before they do the exercise, you may like to read through the grammar box with your students.

🗝 Ticked sentences: 1B, 2A, 3B

Suggested answers:

Mike has already bought a new laptop and found a new job but he hasn't started inline skating yet / learnt how to inline skate yet.

Mary hasn't sold her books on ebay yet. She and Mike haven't got married yet.

5 👥 A nice exercise to get your students to use the target structure (the present perfect with *already* and *yet*) in a natural way. Give them a bit of time to write some more activities and decide whether they have or have not done each one (yet). Then get them to talk to their partner and ask each other questions.

> 📄 **Photocopiable 14** will give your students practice of using *yet* and *already* as well as forming questions with the present perfect.
>
> - Make copies, enough for one between two students, and cut each copy in half.
> - If possible get your students to sit back to back. If that isn't possible, arrange them so they cannot see the other person's paper.
> - Explain to the pairs that they are business partners. They need to call each other and check on progress since they last saw each other.
> - Ideally, they will use the present perfect. If they are struggling, you may like to help them.

6 **2.4** A Sounds good exercise in which your students have to listen out for different intonation. Rising intonation indicates a question.

🗝 1A She's at work?
1B She's at work.
2A She hasn't come home yet.
2B She hasn't come home yet?
3A She can call you on your mobile?
3B She can call you on your mobile.

2.5 Students then listen to the sentences above in context and identify the ones they hear.

🗝 1 B   2 B   3 A

Unit 7 Part B 59

7 The students get some practice of note-taking based on the phone conversation they have just heard. You may need to play the recording more than once.

🔑 Helen from the soup kitchen called. She wants to know if you can work <u>tomorrow evening</u>. She <u>has already asked around</u> | ~~hasn't called anybody else yet~~ and nobody can else can do it. Call her <u>at the soup kitchen</u> | ~~on her mobile~~ as ~~she's already left~~ | <u>she hasn't left yet</u>. The number is 01876 398 123.

8 👥 A nice task for your students: making phone calls and taking messages. It is a fun to arrange them back to back when they do this activity so that they can't see each other (just like a real telephone conversation). True, there will be lots of other people talking, but that is also true of mobile conversations on a crowded train.

9 A final exercise allowing your students to personalize the sentences. This is always a good thing to do so that the grammar is relevant to them.

> **Extension activity:** Get your students to think of things that they would like to do but haven't done … yet. For example: *I would like to go to Kenya – but I haven't been there yet.*

C The winner takes all! coursebook pages 70–71

1 A fun exercise for your students to express themselves using the present perfect.

👥 If you have a large class, you may like to have students work in two groups for the lie-detecting part of exercise.

2 A fun exercise in which the students write the questions as the answers are already given. Below are some suggested answers – or rather, suggested questions.

🔑 2 How many other people have won the prize?
  3 What music is the pianist going to play?/What kind of music have they chosen for the evening?
  4 Where has the company organized similar dinners?
  5 Have any guests ever fallen from their seats?
  6 Have you ever had a dinner in the sky?

3 👥 Another nice activity to get your students talking – this time about competitions they have won. It will perhaps work best if you divide your class into two groups so that at the end they can tell the other group their results.

4 👥 A fun activity for your students and will allow your creative students to shine. Although it is a writing exercise, by doing it in pairs, there will be plenty of speaking as well.

5 A simple exercise giving your students some statements about life that they can agree or disagree with.

    1 home   2 today   3 goals   4 second

6 A look at this unit's **key verb: put**. Your students shouldn't have too much difficulty here.

1 You should put on your hat if you're cold.
2 This is the third time you've put off your holiday this year!
3 Please put away all your books before you leave.
4 They're putting on a play at my child's school next week.
5 How do you put up with all this traffic on your street?

7 **2.6** Your students will hear about Pam and Sam, and get a look at *have been* vs. *have gone*. They should read the statements carefully before they listen.

1 Statement 1 is true. Statement 2 is not true.
2 Statement 1 is completely true. Statement 2 is only half true.

> **Extension activity:** Working in small groups, get your students to mime activities for the others to guess – which will hopefully elicit the present perfect. Examples:
> *Sabine has lost her purse ... and she hasn't found it yet.*
> *Max has eaten too much, but he hasn't been sick yet.*
> *Torsten has asked three girls to marry him, but he hasn't been successful yet.*

8 More practice with the same recording. This time the students take messages. You may need to play the recording more than once.

1 **Jane** called. Call her back on **0163 83 47 165**. It's about **a surprise party for her yoga teacher**.
2 Sam, that was **Henry** on the phone.
His computer **has crashed** but I told him you have really bad **toothache** and you can't talk now. He hopes you **get better/well soon**.

9 **And finally ...** Your students have to unscramble the sentences to form questions and answer them.

1 How many phone messages have you taken today?
2 Have you ever volunteered for anything?
3 What is the most interesting place you have ever visited?
4 How many times have you googled your own name?
5 Who hasn't spoken any German in today's lesson?

8

> **At the end of unit 8 your students should:**
> - know when to use the simple past and when to use the present perfect.
> - be able to talk about the past using *used to*.
> - have picked up vocabulary connected with places to live.
> - have practised too and *not ... enough*.
> - have reviewed prepositions of place and be able to give directions.
> - have studied the key verb *to move*.

A I've moved
coursebook pages 74–75

1 A warmer to introduce your students to the theme of the unit. They have to match up descriptions with photos of places to live. They may not know the word *thatch* though some of your older students will be familiar with the name of the person who works with thatch ...

🔑 1 E 2 C 3 B 4 F 5 A 6 D

Then the students discuss with their partners where they would like to live. Did anyone get any surprises? How many people are perfectly happy where they live at the moment?

2 **2.8** Your students listen to three recordings of people talking about moving house. They have to work out who moved from where to where – and why. Before they listen, you could have them look at the portraits and try to predict the answers.

🔑

	Moved from	Moved to	Because ...
The Greens	a high-rise in a town	a houseboat	they both work from home so can work anywhere.
Patricia Oliver	a cramped bungalow	a remote house with a big garden	she didn't like her cramped bungalow and fell in love with her new place.
The Hudsons	a large semi-detached house 20 miles from the centre	a small flat in a high-rise in the centre of Manchester	Mr Hudson has a new job in the centre of Manchester.

Play the recording again so that they can hear who said the specific sentences.

🔑 The Greens: 3, 6   The Hudsons: 2, 7
    Patricia Oliver: 1, 4, 5, 8

Unit 8 Part A

3 👥 A personalizing exercise in which your students modify the sentences so that they are true for them. They then discuss the differences in the places where they live with their partner. You can then match up pairs with other pairs: pair 1 can explain the differences they have to pair 2, and vice versa.

4 The students complete an email from Trish to Mike, adding the correct verb forms. They may find the information in the grammar box useful.

🔑
- 1 haven't found
- 2 have just had
- 3 told
- 4 converted
- 5 have just read
- 6 bought
- 7 renovated/have renovated

The students also have to look out for examples of *too ...* and *not ... enough* in the email.

🔑 too expensive, too dull, too difficult, not big enough

5 👥 The students match up the descriptions with the photos. The answers are based on the students' opinions so no answer key here.

> 📄 Use **photocopiable 15** to give your students more practice of *too ...* and *not ... enough*.
>
> - Make one copy for each group of about 4–5 students. Cut out the 12 cards for each group. Keep the 'cheat sheet' separate.
> - Arrange your students in groups of about 4–5 with a table in the middle. Put the cards, face down, on the table.
> - You may like to model the exercise first. You can take one of the cards and read it out. Then invite your students to respond. Encourage, but don't force them, to use the target structures, *too ...* and *not ... enough*.
> - Once you have modelled the exercise, you can get them to work in their groups. One student reads out the card and the others respond.
> - Give your weaker students the 'cheat sheet' with the adjectives they might like to use. Your stronger students should be able to cope without it.

6 The students are introduced to the language of estate agents – English style! They have to match up the descriptions given with reality.

🔑 1 C   2 B   3 D   4 A

Afterwards they can work in pairs to write one-sentence descriptions of their own homes. You can have them write one colourful and one standard version.

B The good old days

coursebook pages 76-77

1 In this warmer your students discuss the descriptions and decide which ones describe the place they lived in when they were children.

2 A reading comprehension. Your students will read about Moira who emigrated to Australia in 1990. They then do a True/False exercise. They should check the answers with each other before they check them with you.

🔑 1 F   2 T   3 F   4 F

3 A multiple choice exercise based on the text the students have just read. The students may notice that the structure *used to* pops up a few times.

🔑 1 near Loch Ness   3 cold   5 on the stage
    2 opposite   6 so many tourists

In the feedback session it might be useful to get the students to think about the *used to* structure. For example, once they have established that the answer number 1 is 'Loch Ness' you can ask: *Does she live near Loch Ness now? (No.) Did she live near Loch Ness in the past? (Yes.) Did she live near Loch Ness for a short time or quite a long time? (Quite a long time.)* This will help them establish when *used to* should be used. Note that the negative *I didn't use to ...* and the question form *Did you use to ...?* are both quite rare.

4 👥 A quick exercise for the students to practise *used to*. They can complete the sentences in any way they like so the examples below are just suggestions.

🔑 1 When I was young, I used to steal apples from my neighbour's garden.
    2 I never used to like gardening but now I grow all my own vegetables.
    3 My car used to break down a lot but now it runs beautifully.
    4 Did you use to fight with your sister when you were a child?
    5 Did your grandparents use to give you money?

📄 Use **photocopiable 16** to give your students some more practice with *used to*.

- Make a copy and cut the out the cards, keeping the sentence beginnings and endings in two separate piles. Mix each pile well.
- Distribute the beginnings to one half of the class and the endings to the other. (If you have a small class, you can leave the piles at the front of the class and have students do multiple rounds, selecting their own cards each time.)
- Students then mingle and search for the other half of their sentence. Make sure they speak to each other, not just show their cards. Once they find their match, they can sit down (or select another card and do another round).

5 Still with a Scottish theme, your students can practise their prepositions.

🔑   1 opposite (not *opposite to*!)   3 betweens
       2 next to   4 past, along

6 **2.9** A listening comprehension. Your students listen to Martin asking some questions at the Tourist Information Centre. They can find some of the places he mentions on the map.

🔑 He asks about Calton Hill, but St James Centre and Leith are mentioned too.

The students also have to work out which things have changed in Edinburgh and which things are still the same.

🔑   1 The view is the same

     2 The place where people go skateboarding has changed. They used to go down Calton Hill but now they go to Transgression Park in Leith.

     3 The numbers of shoppers has increased.

     4 The weather is the same.

7 👥 The students practise giving directions using the map of Edinburgh, either in pairs or, if you prefer, in small groups. One person chooses a destination, but doesn't tell the others which one. They then follow the directions given and try to work out where the instructions lead them. If the students are having problems, you may like to model the task for them.

Once they have worked on the Edinburgh examples, perhaps with some help from the information in the box, they can practise on some local examples. They shouldn't say where they are 'directing' people. The others should try to work out the destination.

C   Things have changed   coursebook pages 78–79

1 👥 A 'find someone who' exercise to get your students to practise the *used to* structure and the present perfect. Encourage them to talk to as many different people as possible.

2 An exercise which will test your students' 'knowledge' of English village life. We can't expect them to know the answers but they can discuss the questions with their classmates.

🔑   1 'Proper' pubs are in decline in Britain. The smoking ban means that many smokers now drink at home and many pubs are going out of business.

     2 Church attendance is also in decline. Many churches offer other social activities in a village, coffee mornings, play groups etc.

     3 Probably not, though this might be changing.

     4 A good village postmaster (or postmistress) will know all the local residents, though the post office is also in decline with many of them now sharing premises with a grocer's.

5 Village greens and duck ponds are still quite common – at least those that haven't been turned into car parks!

They then check the map to see what they can find there. You might want to take this opportunity to practise prepositions of place. Can they tell you where everything is?

🔑 The village has two pubs, a church, a post office and a duck pond. It even has an internet cafe with wifi (wireless internet access).

3 More practice of giving directions. The students have to add the missing words to the text. Get them to work together on this one.

🔑   1 far   4 ahead   7 opposite
     2 straight   5 past
     3 second   6 right

2.10 👥 After they listen to the recording to check their answers, students work in pairs to give each other directions on how to get to different places in the village. It is best if they keep the destination a secret so the others have to work it out.

4 A reading comprehension about the village of Poundbury. You can get your students to mention the good and bad points about living there and write them on the board. They can then make up their own opinion as to why they would, or wouldn't, like to live there.

🔑 **Poundbury's good points**   **Poundbury's bad points**
It's in a nice area.   Very few road signs.
Lots of footpaths and cycle lanes.   No traditional old buildings.
No ugly TV aerials on the roofs.   Limited employment prospects.

5 **2.11** Your students will hear Louis talking about life in Poundbury compared to his life in Edinburgh. Give them time to look at the table before you play the recording.

🔑

	Poundbury	**Edinburgh**
Population	6000 (this information is in the text in exercise 4)	Half a million
People	Quiet, difficult to get to know the people	Laid back / relaxed
Night life	Nothing to do. A bit dull, totally dead.	Lots of bars and shows
Buildings	No restaurants, take-aways, cinemas, theatres, petrol stations.	Great shops and restaurants
Unique features	Very strange place	Best nightlife in UK

Finally the students should compare Louis' life in Edinburgh with his life in Poundbury. They will come up with many examples. Here are some suggestions.

1 He used to be a lot happier in Edinburgh. He finds Poundbury a bit dull.
2 He used to live in a flat. Now he lives in a house.
3 He used to enjoy his evenings. Now he does overtime at work.
4 He used to know a lot of people. Now he knows almost no one.

6 With some help from the text, the students can fill in the table. This should a revision exercise as they probably know these structures already.

things	people	places
something	somebody	somewhere
nothing	nobody	nowhere
anything	anybody	anywhere
everything	everybody	everywhere

Now they fill in the missing word in the sentences.

1 something
2 nobody
3 somewhere
4 everywhere
5 everybody

7 Your students get more practice with the **key verb move**. They will hopefully come up with some creative sentences.

Model answers:

1 Look – I have just moved my car so that you can park more easily.
2 When I was a child, we moved from Hildesheim to Heidelberg.
3 A neighbour of mine moved into his boyfriend's flat.
4 One of the most moving moments in my life was the first time my stepson called me 'daddy'.
5 A member of my family once moved out after we couldn't agree about money.

8 Your students write three things about themselves, two of which are true, one of which is a complete lie. When they read out their three sentences, the others in the group can ask questions to find out which one is not true.

Journal II

See notes in the teaching tips (page 10) on ways to use the material in the journals.

Coursebook pages 82–89

Air Travel 101

Before reading
- Your students get into groups and think of the best airport they have ever visited and the best airline they have every flown with. (It is quite likely they will also discuss the worst airport and airline as well.) They can then share their ideas with the group.

After reading
- Ask half the class to note down the things that impressed Lisa about Changi Airport. The other half should note down the things that impressed her about Emirates Air. They then add more ideas which could have been on the list, but weren't. Then they read out the list to the other group, who try to detect which items are genuine and which were made up.

Mission ... possible

Before reading
- Get your students to look at the picture. Who is the first person to notice something special about the picture? (The fact that the people sitting across from each other on the subway are identical twins.)

After reading
- **My favourite**: In the article, your students can read about four of the ideas organized by 'Improv Everywhere'. Which one is their favourite and why? They can discuss this in groups.
- **Hey, we could do that:** The students brainstorm to think of some new ideas for 'Improv Everywhere', or, if they want to, something they could do themselves. The crazier the ideas the better, but they should bring a smile to people's lives. ?

Sleep well! ...

Before reading
- Your students discuss what they need for a good night's sleep. Do they have any tips for anyone who has problems sleeping?

After reading
- **Which photo?** In small groups, one student chooses a photo. The others ask questions to find out which photo it is – using as few questions as possible. For example: *Can you see a window in the photo? Is there more than one bed in the photo?* The student who correctly identifies the photo gets to choose the next one. ?
- **Linking**: It is very common for native speakers, though not so common for learners, to use linking, in which the last sound of one word merges into the first sound of the next word,

e. g.: *Than kyou, thi smorning, a norange.* It is not easy to get your students to start linking but a useful activity is to get them to be aware of it. Ask them to go through the text and find places where they think linking can occur. They can discuss this in small groups and then as a class. Do they agree on which words can be linked?

Not just words

Before reading
- Ask your students about the game Scrabble: *Have you played it before? Do you have a set at home? Have you ever played it in an unusual place?* Before they look at the page (though they may have seen it already) can they imagine some crazy places where you could play Scrabble? Get them to brainstorm some great ideas before sharing them with the group.

After reading
- **That's a long one!:** Generally, long words score more than short words in Scrabble. What is the longest word they can find in the text? (The answer is 'distribution', with 12 letters). What is the longest English word your students can think of (without using a dictionary)? (Most authorities accept that, with 45 letters, the longest word in English is 'pneumonoultramicroscopicsilicovolcanoconiosis', a lung disease, though your students probably won't come up with that one!

City break: Istanbul

Before reading
- Get your students to discuss what they know about Istanbul and what they would like to know about Istanbul. While they are reading they can check to confirm their ideas, or, hopefully, get the answers to some of their questions.

After reading
- **History:** A number of events in the history of Istanbul are mentioned in the text. Can you students put them in chronological order? They can work in small groups – and then compare their list with that of another group.

- **We can do that here:** The students discuss the things (mentioned in the article) which can be done both in Istanbul and their own town.

It's in the stars

Before reading
- Ask your students: *Do you read your horoscopes?* and *Do you believe that horoscopes can really predict our future?*

After reading
- **Brainstorming:** Your students will probably have different views about Miriam and her attitude to horoscopes. Let them come up with a variety of adjectives which they feel describe Miriam. They then divide them into three groups: positive, neutral and negative adjectives. They can compare their adjectives with those of the other groups.

9

> **At the end of unit 9 your students should:**
> - be able to talk about technology.
> - have studied the *will*-future.
> - have practised a range of time adverbials.
> - have reviewed a wide variety of tenses.
> - have discussed future developments and be able to describe trends.

A I'll show you
coursebook pages 90–91

1 A Your students discuss what household appliances they have at home, and how often they use them. Then they discuss which one/s they could live without. The students may like to mention other appliances they have which are not on the list. A nice way to get them practising their time adverbials without realizing!

2 A quick quiz for your students so that they find out if they are technophiles or technophobes. Monitor the class while they are carrying out the activity as they may need your help with some of the vocabulary. They get feedback from the quiz on page 131 and it might be interesting to discuss whether they agree with the findings of the test – or not.

3 A quick tense review with the help of a short text about an English guy and his Japanese girlfriend.

1 am
2 don't go
3 have even started
4 haven't finished
5 is definitely getting
6 was speaking
7 understood
8 are flying/are going to fly

4 A nice 'find someone who' which involves a range of tenses and some interesting questions about gadgets. In the feedback session, don't ask your students for everything they found out: just ask a few people for something which surprised them or that they would like to share with the group.

5 **2.13** Listening comprehension. Your students listen to two short dialogues. They have to work out what items are being used, and why.

a tape measure — to measure the size of David's bag.
scales — to weigh the bag
an iron — to melt the wax
toilet paper — probably to absorb the wax, but we don't know for sure

Unit 9 Part A

You may need to play the recording again to allow your students the chance to hear whether the sentences given were in the recording. Let them debate it before you play it again.

🔑 1, 3, 5, 6, 7, 10, 12

6 Some short dialogues to help your students with using *shall, wi*ll and *won't*. Note that *shall* is more common in British English than in both Irish and American English.

🔑 1 Shall, close
'll, put on
2 Shall, make
'll, drink
3 won't start
'll be

> Use **photocopiable 17** and **18** to give your students practice of using the spontaneous *will*-future.

- Make copies of both photocopiables. Cut up the 'Help! Help!' cards and put them, face down, on the front desk. Cut up the gadget cards, and hand them out to the students. Instruct them not to look at them until you say so.
- Model the activity for your students. Take a 'Help! Help!' card and read it out, adding *Can you help me ... ?* and the name of one of the students. The chosen student then looks at the gadget he/she has and thinks of what he/she can do with it to help.
For example:
Teacher: *Help! Help! I have a very young baby and she needs special care. Can you help me ... Natalie?*
Natalie: *I have a microwave oven. I'll make some warm milk for the baby.*
- If the exercise looks like it will go on for too long, you could hand out the 'Help! Help!' cards and get students to find a suitable matches. This should still be done orally, not just by showing the cards to each other.

7 Your students get practice responding to text messages. As they have to react spontaneously, they will (hopefully) use the *will*-future.

🔑 Suggested answers:

1 Our teacher is wonderful! Shall we buy her a holiday in the Caribbean? I'll get some brochures.
2 I'll call the AA. (The Automobile Association, not Alcoholics Anonymous!)
3 I'll buy them off you!
4 I'll cancel our skiing holiday and I'll come and see you tomorrow.

B Change happens

coursebook pages 92–93

1 A fun brainstorming activity in which your students think of products which match the descriptions. They then draw pictures of the products. A nice way to manage this is for you to collect two or three drawings from each group. We are definitely not looking for good artwork. In fact, some ambiguity is more likely to generate dialogue!

> Model answers:
> 1 a big bar of chocolate
> 2 a games console
> 3 a treadmill
> 4 a bicycle

2 Looking to the future. The students work in pairs to rank a number of futuristic ideas in order of how likely they think they are. Once they've finished, they can compare their ranking (orally) with another pair. For those students unfamiliar with Star Trek, a beamer can make someone disappear in one place, and reappear in another.

3 2.14 A listening comprehension in which three people talk about the future on a radio programme. Play the recording once and give your students time to discuss what they heard. Then get them to do the matching exercise, for which they don't actually need the recording, though they will need it to say in which time period the prediction was for.

> 1 C [m]   4 E [m]
> 2 B [c]   5 A [c]
> 3 F [d]   6 D [c]

4 The students read some predictions from a website and discuss which ones they agree or disagree with. They then have the opportunity to make predictions of their own.

5 Students match various questions to the topic areas. There are a number of possible answers which should generate some healthy debate.

> 1 transportation, environment, technology
> 2 environment, technology, health
> 3 health, environment
> 4 food, health
> 5 fashion
> 6 technology, environment, health

6 👥 They should then answer the questions with their partner – which again, should bring about a healthy debate.

6 👥 The students choose one of the topics – one that interests them – and write some questions about the past, the present and the future. Help your students at this stage so that they have good questions to work with.

👥 When they are ready, they should stand up, move around, and talk to as many people as possible, asking them one or two questions each, and making a note of the responses.

In the feedback session, ask a few people for some interesting answers they received. They should try to use some of the language in the box.

7 Some surprising predictions, some of which your students may know but they should be able to work out if they don't. Allow them to work together.

🔑
1 television
2 computers
3 cinema
4 iPod

8 👥 And finally, the students talk in pairs about their own hopes for the future. Listen in on the conversations and, in the feedback session, ask them to share interesting hopes and dreams that they heard.

C Getting better

coursebook pages 94–95

1 A warm-up activity to get your students using the *will*-future (and some key verbs) in a light-hearted way.

🔑 Model answers:
1 a marathon
2 even more beautiful
3 your shoes off
4 for the government

In the feedback session, don't forget to ask about the extra predictions they made and whether their partner agreed with them or not.

2 The students have to make choices as to which things they prefer. This will generate a healthy debate and also introduce the vocabulary for the next exercise.

3   A reading comprehension. The students read an interesting text about Zambikes, a company in Zambia that makes bikes, then answer some questions.

- 1 False. Zambikes is a Zambian company.
- 2 True
- 3 True
- 4 False. The company will sell their bikes in the US.
- 5 True
- 6 True
- 7 True

4   A review of tenses in the form of twitter updates. Allow your students to work together on this one.

- 1 needs
- 2 is riding
- 3 is sending
- 4 built
- 5 sent
- 6 has just produced
- 7 is

5   Questions about Africa. The students write down any questions they have about Africa – then try to find someone to answer them. Knowing the answer is not important; it is the discussion that the activity generates that counts.

6   Matching questions and answers with the **key verb get**. Encourage the students to use the key verb as much as possible so that they 'own' the word.

    1 C   2 E   3 B   4 A   5 F   6 D

7   Students work in pairs to convince each other to buy the products pictured. Have them read through the example and sample sentence beginnings first.

8   A lead-up to a **sounds good** exercise on contractions. Get one student to read the text to another. Can either of them guess what Bob is describing?

2.15 In part two they'll hear Bob. They should listen out for the differences between the text and what Bob actually says. Can they hear how much more natural it sounds with the contractions?

⚙ I've just bought a new one because my old one **didn't** work anymore. I hope the new one'll be OK. I think it**'ll** be simple to use but I have**n't** read the instructions yet. But I**'m** sure I **won't** get lost so easily again!

9 👥 A group writing exercise – writing a text about a gadget. They should give some clues but nothing too obvious. Then they should them read them out. Can the other students guess what it is?

10 **And finally ...** Personalizing some sentences based on the material found in the unit.

10

> **At the end of unit 10 your students should:**
> - be able to use *when, as soon as, before, after* and *not ... until*.
> - have looked at the difference between *going to* and the *will*-future.
> - have reviewed sports and leisure activities.
> - be able to use *if* clauses and have practised *when* and *if* sentences.
> - have practised making appointments.
> - have studied the key verb *give*.

A Be part of it!
coursebook pages 98–99

1 Your students discuss various sports and leisure activities and decide whether you *do, go,* or *play* them. Tell them that some items fit more than one category.

	do	aerobics, weightlifting, yoga, the gardening, cycling, a sponsored walk, wii fit
	go	swimming, on a safari, bowling, fishing, on a pilgrimage, skating, on a sponsored walk
	play	chess, golf, cards, the piano, hockey, monopoly, wii fit

2 **2.17** A listening comprehension. Your students will listen to Edith, Terry and Paul talk about the sports they do – and used to do.

	Edith	used to go on long hikes, now does ballroom dancing.
	Terry	cycles to work, uses a wii fit, might join a fitness studio later.
	Paul	usually plays football, though not at the moment. He is playing board games while his ankle is broken.

In the second part of the exercise, students have to make logical sentences based on the recording.

1 Edith forgets her age as soon as the music starts.
2 Terry will get a personal trainer when the moment is right.
3 Paul won't start drinking beer until his friend arrives.

3 A nice personalizing exercise. If students need some help with the structures, they can look at the grammar box.

The students then compare their sentences. Encourage them to do this orally rather than simply by exchanging lists.

> **Photocopiable 19** will give your students more practice of the structure *until*.
> - Make enough copies so each student has a cartoon. Cut out the cards.
> - Explain that you will give them one cartoon each. They should show it to their classmates, who should tell them what the person is saying after the word 'no'.
> - They should make a note of any interesting/clever/funny answers they get.
> - If you think the students will have problems, you could use one cartoon as an example (you can enlarge it on the photocopier) and help them with a possible answer.
> Suggested answers:
> *You can't play football until ...*　　*You can't walk across the floor until ...*
> *I won't let you kiss me until ...*　　*Don't try to use the computer until ...*
> *You can't have any dessert until ...*　*Don't unfasten your seatbelt until ...*
> *You can't buy any beer until ...*　　*You can't go skiing until until ...*

4 A quick collocation exercise with *raise, make, do, play, take* and *get*. This conveniently introduces vocabulary needed for exercise 5.

   1 raise money/children/~~a challenge~~
   2 make ~~photographs~~/money/a difference
   3 do something fun/extraordinary things/~~a difference~~
   4 play a ~~marathon~~/a charity match/an exciting game
   5 take place/~~a challenge~~/ten hours
   6 get active/involved/~~a difference~~

5 A reading exercise about Sport Relief in the UK. The students then correct some false statements about the event.

   1 Sport Relief raises money for **vulnerable people**.
   2 **Some** of the people who take part are celebrities. **Many are ordinary people.**
   3 The event takes place **every other year/every two years**.
   4 They **still** give the money to poor people in the UK and abroad.

6 Group discussion. In small groups, the students discuss events similar to Sport Relief in their own country using the questions as a guide. They may like to consider both national events as well as small scale events, perhaps ones that they have participated in.

7 Your students can choose three activities they would like to do to raise money. Once completed, they can discuss the possibilities with their partners.

> **Extension activity:** The students can try to guess which options were chosen by various members of the group. Were they right? You don't need to ask the whole group – about three should be enough.

8 👥 A nice brainstorming activity which will hopefully generate some interesting and creative ideas.

9 👥 *And finally ...* A nice, relaxed way to end the lesson. Students get a chance to tell their partners about their own favourite sport or hobby.

B Give it a go!

coursebook pages 100–101

1 A brainstorming activity to get the students thinking about sports and games. Below you can see some suggested answers:

🔑 no equipment needed: yoga, tai chi
a bit expensive: yachting, golf
quite unusual: juggling, curling
thrilling: bobsleigh, skiing
too tiring: rock climbing, marathon running

Encourage students to ask as many people as possible about the activities. In the feedback session ask for unusual activities and also any surprising answers.

2 A reading exercise about fitness. This should generate plenty of debate. No answers here as it up to the students to decide.

3 A matching exercise using examples of the first conditional based on the text in part 2. If your students have problems, get them to look at the grammar box.

🔑   1 B   2 D   3 C   4 E   5 F   6 A

4 👥 A nice brainstorming activity in which your students come up with some gym-free and fun fitness challenges. (Note that *gym* is short for *gymnasium* and is used here as an alternative to *health club* or *fitness centre*.) They then swap cards with another group and make comments about the ideas. Encourage them to look at the example sentences so that they (hopefully) use the first conditional in their responses.

> Use **photocopiable 20** to give your students more practice of the first conditional and of sports equipment.
>
> - Make a copy and cut up the sport and equipment cards.
> - Ask for five sporty volunteers (they don't really have to be sporty) and give them the sport cards. Explain that to do their sport, they will need some equipment.
> - Hand out the equipment cards to the other people. The equipment people should gather around the volunteers, about four per person.
> - The volunteers must not name their sport. But they can talk about it.
>   For example: I'm going to the Alps this weekend to do my sport. *I'm going with my friend Rheinhold Messner ...*
>   Equipment person: *Aha, if you're going rock climbing, you'll need ... some rope!*
> - The activity ends when all the volunteers have all the equipment (four items) they need. If your students are competitive, you can make it a race.

5 **2.18** Students listen to a telephone call in which a man answers an advertisement for a private poker trainer.

⚷	Reason for call:	Angela wants to hire Pete to give her husband poker lessons for his birthday.
	Caller's name:	Peter – or Pete – Larsson
	Caller's job:	retired, but used to work in a casino. Now he gives private poker lessons.
	Place to meet:	at Angela's house (24 Rosetree Drive)
	Appointment time:	Wednesday at 2.30 pm

In the second exercise, students tick the correct endings to the *if* sentence.

⚷ Correct sentence endings: 2 and 6

6 The students unscramble a dialogue on making an appointment before reading it out together.

⚷ Right order: B – E – G – D – F – A – C

7 Your students get practice making appointments. They should try to talk to as many people as possible to fill up their diary. They have plenty of support from the example sentence and the language box.

8 **And finally ...** The students discuss various scenarios with their partners (and hopefully make a lot of nice conditional 1 statements). Make sure you monitor your students and give them any support they need.

C Going for gold

coursebook pages 102–103

1 A quick exercise on unusual sports and where they originated. The students should not feel bad if they don't know where the sports originated – or even if they have never heard of the sports!

🔑
sumo wrestling	Japan
taekwondo	Korea
cheese rolling	England
sled-dog racing	USA
kabbadi	India
ice hockey	Canada
mobile-phone throwing	Finland

👥 The students can then find out as much as they can about each sport from other people in the class.

2 A bit of grammar and a bit of detective work for your students to work out the Olympic venues that are being described.

🔑
1 held, were	Barcelona
2 hosted, 've held	Athens
3 were flying, lit/lighted	London
4 is sinking, has hosted	Mexico City

3 A reading comprehension about a woman who lives near the Olympic stadium in London. If you're using the book after 2012, then you will know more about the London Olympics. You can still do the exercise, just explain to your students that the interview took place in 2010 – before the Olympics.

🔑
1 if   3 if/when   5 if
2 when   4 when   6 when

4 Probably best to get your students to work in pairs on this one. The debate how many people will fall into the various groups. Then they ask their classmates to find out how accurate they were.

Unit 10 Part C

5 **Key verb: give.** The students complete the questions and then match them up with the answers.

> 1 C giving, a lift
> 2 D Have, given
> 3 A give
> 4 E give, back
> 5 B have, given

👥 They can then ask their partners the same questions.

6 **2.19** Listening comprehension. Your students listen to a dialogue between Keith and June and have to find out what they are going to organize – and why.

> They are planning a day at the races to celebrate Andy's 50th birthday.

In the second part of the exercise, students have to fill in a short exercise, before they listen to the recording again to check their answer.

> 1 Before   4 after
> 2 until   5 as soon as
> 3 after

7 👥 **And finally ...** Your students get to look back through the unit to find countries and cities. They then use one of the target structures, the first conditional, to talk about what they'll do if they visit the places they've chosen.

> **Extension exercise:** As a follow up and a nice way to contrast *will* and *going to*, tell the students that you have granted their wish and they will all go to the places they've chosen. Now that they are definitely going to whatever city or country they've picked, they can tell the class what they *are going to do* there, using *going to* for plans.

11

At the end of unit 11 your students should:
- have looked at a variety of shops and discussed products and prices.
- have practised the present perfect with *for* and *since*.
- have practised making comparisons with *(not) as ... as*.
- have practised the modal verb *might*.
- have looked at linking words.
- have enjoyed talking about films

A I'll take it!

coursebook pages 92–93

1 Your students do a quick quiz which will help them debate their attitudes towards shopping. No answer key here as this is simply to encourage discussion.

2 A vocabulary boosting exercise in which the students decide where certain products are normally bought. Note that some things can be bought in more than one shop.

a pharmacy	herbal tea, cough medicine, hair dryer, shampoo
a department store	depending on the store, it could be everything, except cough medicine and an iPad perhaps.
a stationery shop	wrapping paper, highlighters, postcards, balloons, birthday cards
an electronics shop	a laptop, hair dryer, iPad, a video camera, DVD

3 **2.21** A listening comprehension exercise in which Sandy and Luke are trying to buy something. The students should listen carefully and fill in the table.

	Sandy	Luke
what?	a hairdryer	a CD
for whom?	her husband	his mother-in-law
how much?	final price, £34.99	£31.98
which shop?	could be a pharmacy, an electronics shop or a department store	probably a department store (because both perfume and CDs are sold)

4 A nice dialogue exercise in which the students sort out the right order of a dialogue between a shopper and a shop assistant.

1 D   2 G   3 C   4 I   5 E   6 F   7 A   8 H   9 B

Once they have found the right order, students can make their own dialogue. Encourage them to use some of the phrases in the language box.

> Use **photocopiable 21** to give your students the opportunity to discuss products that they have bought in a humorous role-play.

- Cut out the 21 cards and put them in a bag.
- Before starting the activity, model it by asking one of your students, preferably one of the opposite sex, to come to the front of the class.
- Explain to the group that you and Student A have been married (or just good friends) for a long time and are happy, but very, very poor. You went to the market this morning and student A bought something. Have Student A take a card from the bag and tell the group what he/she bought.
- Now comment on student A's purchase and ask him/her to defend the purchase.
  You: *So Dietlind, what did you buy at the market?*
  Dietlind: *I bought ... a piece of Madonna's hair!*
  You: *What? I don't understand it. Dietlind, we are poor, very poor. You know we only eat bread and sauerkraut. Why did you buy a piece of Madonna's hair?*
  Dietlind: *I bought it for you. I know how much you love Madonna. I wanted to make you happy.*
- Split the students into groups of 4–6. Let them form couples (or just friends), choose cards and take turns playing the roles of the two poor people in front of their group. The person who purchased the object should try to find as many reasons for buying it as possible (including what one can use the object for).

5 The students look at some items on eBay and discuss what price they think the items will finally sell for. The should do this in groups before a final feedback session. You may have to explain what amber is.

6 First of all the students read Nina's email to find out which item mentioned in exercise 5 she is selling.

🔑 She is selling the vase.

In the second part of the exercise, the students match up sentence halves where the emphasis is on present perfect with *for* and *since*.

🔑 1 C   2 A   3 D   4 B

7 A class survey in which the students ask each other some questions about online auctions – and conveniently practise the present perfect at the same time.

8 Some more practice of the present perfect in which the students have to add the correct form of the verb and the words *for* or *since*. There are a number of possible answers so the answers below are just suggestions.

🔑
1 have been, for
2 has been, for
3 have known, since
4 have had, since
5 has lived, since

The students then personalize the sentences by changing them so that they are true for them.

9 Students finish the lesson by asking each other *How long?* questions. They have some useful prompts in the boxes but shouldn't feel limited to these questions. Just in case some students ask some inappropriate questions, you might like to remind them of the phrase: *I'd rather not answer that.*

B Money matters

coursebook pages 108–109

1 A simple exercise to get your students to think about vocabulary connected with money: find the odd one out. Note that students often confuse *borrow* and *lend*.

1 earn (with the others you lose money in some way)
2 auction (the others are something of monetary value)
3 borrow (with all the others you give something away)
4 generous (the others indicate the value of something)

2 The students have probably heard of Audrey Hepburn and Oprah Winfrey but almost certainly don't know Jane Ritchie. The important part of this exercise is the contrast between talking about someone who is still alive (Oprah) with someone who is no longer with us (Audrey). The students should notice the similarity between sentence 1 and sentence 2, for example, but also the very important difference.

1 Oprah   3 Oprah   5 Audrey
2 Audrey   4 Jane   6 Oprah

3 A reading exercise based on Jane Ritchie, the woman in exercise 2. Students first determine the significance of the numbers.

30   Margery Freeman's husband died 30 years ago.
59   Jane's age when she inherited the money.
101   The age at which Margery Freeman died.
9 m   The amount of money Jane inherited.

In the second part of the exercise, they decide whether the statements are true or false.

1 False. Margery Freeman was her (distant) cousin.
2 True
3 False. She has bought very little and given most of the money to charity.
4 True
5 Answer depends on the current year.

> Use **photocopiable 22** to give you students some practice of fundraising skills.
>
> - Make a copy and cut out the eight cards. If you have a large group, you can use all the cards. If you have a smaller group, you can leave some of the cards out. Ideally there should be 2–3 students in each group.
> - Explain that you have eight (less if you use fewer cards) million pounds to help a number of charities. Each charity needs support and they have to give a one minute presentation on why their charity should be supported.
> - After the presentations, each group decides how 1 million pounds should be divided. They cannot give money to their own presentation.
> - Find out which charity is going to get the most money – which may be because it is a worthwhile charity though no doubt helped by a good presentation.

4 The students read some statements about money which all contain the target structure *(not) as ... as*. They can debate the phrases with their partners before making some more sentences (not necessarily about money) using the target structure. There are some useful adjectives in the box though they don't need to limit themselves to these words. Below are some suggested answers.

  1 I'm not as lucky as my brother. He's won the lottery three times!
  2 I'm only as old as I look – which means I'm 79.
  3 My ex-boyfriend is not as interesting as my new one!

5 **2.22** A listening comprehension in which the students listen to an interview with Jack about his rags to riches story and the many jobs he has had

  dog walker, door-to-door salesman, busker, cook, house-cleaner, artist

The students then use the table to produce true statements. There are many possibilities so the ones below are just suggestions

  Kerry might not be interested in buying the watch after all.
  Jack might go to South Africa next month.
  People might be interested in buying Jack's paintings.

6 A question and answer session in pairs or small groups based on future plans and possibilities. No answer key as the students can give their own answers.

7 And finally, the students debate the relative value of a number of items. The object here it to generate debate rather than have the 'real' answers, but here are some approximate values: Audrey Hepburn stamp, 70,000 euros; Fleurburger (made with Kobe beef and topped with fois gras and truffles), 3,700 euros; Jimmy Choo shoes, 600 euros; fake Rolex watch, 25 euros.

C It was worth it!

coursebook pages 110–111

1 A *quick quiz* to get your students thinking about India. We are not expecting your students to know the answers but they can debate what they think is the right answer.

🔑 1 rupees (the Indian currency) 3 polo
    2 tiger   4 Indian State Railways

2 Your students read a text about the popular film, 'Slumdog Millionaire', and add the linking words. Note that some of the linking words are used more than once.

🔑 1 and   3 because   5 then   7 so
    2 But   4 so   6 But   8 When

3 The students have to put the paragraph in the correct order. Let them work together as this might be a little tricky for them.

🔑 1 A 2 C 3 E 4 G 5 B 6 D 7 I 8 H 9 F

👥 The students can then give their partners a very short summary (preferably in four sentences) of a film they have seen recently. Can the partners guess the name of the film?

4 👥 The students ask and answer various questions, which all require the present perfect. You may like to check they can do the first one before they work on their own.

🔑 1 How many times have you seen Slumdog Millionaire?
    2 How long have you been a movie fan?
    3 How many episodes of the millionaire show have you watched?
    4 How long have you had your watch?
    5 How long have you been awake so far today?
    6 How many times have you been to an English-speaking country?

5 **2.23** A listening comprehension in which the students listen to Karl talking about his experiences in Mumbai.

🔑 He's calling Donna, who's his colleague, because he wants her to join him in Mumbai.

You can either play the recording again before students do the second part of the exercise or let them work in pairs or small groups to see how much they remember about these six topics before listening to check.

🔑 1 traffic   crazy
    2 food   hot, but not as hot as the Indian restaurant in Covent Garden
    3 weather   a bit hotter than he expected, it sometimes buckets down (rains a lot)
    4 shopping   a lot of fun, incredible bazaars, street markets
    5 people   the crowds are crazy, talkative,

Unit 11 Part C

    6 prices   cheaper than in London

6 Your students compare different countries that they are familiar with and share information. The two model sentences should help them. No answer key as they will come up with their own ideas.

> Use **photocopiable 23** to give your students the opportunity to role-play a scene in a shop. This is something for the thespians in the group. If you have any very shy students, let them restrict their involvement to 'backstage', i.e., to writing or organizing props.
>
> - Make a copy and cut out the cards. (There are six in all.)
> - Divide your class into six groups. (Ideally there should be 3–4 people in each group. If you have a smaller class, you could use fewer cards.)
> - Explain that you are a film director and you are looking for some new stars for your latest films. Each group has just ten minutes (but be flexible enough to allow more time if needed) to prepare a short scene and all the information they need for the scene is written on the cards.
> - Hand out the cards, one per group, and start the clock. Go around to each group and help them with the writing (or planning) if they ask for it.
> - After the ten minutes, get each group to come up and perform their scene. The audience could guess what type of scene they have acted (as given in the headline of each card). If you feel your group is a particularly serious one that would feel uncomfortable acting, then they could simply write the dialogue and read it out.
> - If you have a video camera, that would be a nice touch, but don't worry if you don't have one. Make sure there is plenty of applause at the end of each scene – and of course they are all winners.

7 **Key verb: spend.** The students add nouns and verbs related to money in three sentences. There are different possible answers so the ones below are just suggestions.

    me, has lost   some time, borrow   shoes, saving

8 A fun activity in which your students compare how they spend their time and money. This should be done in small groups before a feedback session with the whole class. Are there any surprises?

9 **And finally ...** The students try to answer some of the questions that Jamal answered in 'Slumdog Millionaire'. Note that the numbering is taken from the film: these were the fifth, seventh and ninth (and final) questions.

    5 Benjamin Franklin   7 London   9 Aramis

The students then work in pairs to write a quiz question for another pair of students in the class.

Journal III

See notes in the teaching tips (page 10) on ways to use the material in the journals.

Coursebook pages 114–121

My fellow Americans

Before reading
- Your students get into groups and let them discuss the positive and negative stereotypes of Americans abroad. It will be interesting to see which list is longer!

After reading
- **Europe and America**: Ask the students to compare the generalizations that Lisa mentions, with their own feelings about Europeans. One example: "Americans are very confident." How do Europeans compare?

What a waste!

Before reading
- Ask the students to discuss their views of modern art and whether there are any artists that they particularly like (or dislike).
- Get the students to discuss how much waste people in their country throw away. Is it more or less than in other countries?

After reading
- **Next project**: The students can discuss what other waste material Chris Jordan could use for his next piece of art. They write a list of different ideas. They then hand the list to another group who discuss what Chris Jordan should make with the various materials. How creative are your students?

- **Hey, we could do that:** The students brainstorm to think of some new ideas for 'Improv Everywhere', or, if they want to, something they could do themselves. The crazier the ideas the better, but they should bring a smile to people's lives. ?

- **Internet:** Those of your students with an internet connection may like to look at Chris Jordan's other work. Can they report back next week for those who don't have an internet connection?

Turtle Bay

This is one of my favourite images in the journals and I think your students will love it as well. It is likely to generate discussion among the students but here are a few ideas as to how you may like to exploit the Turtle Bay pages.

Before reading
- Your students share their experiences of turtles, and what they know about turtles. *Have you ever seen one in the wild? In a zoo? On television? What kind of animals are they? Where do they live?* Lots of things for them to discuss.
- Marijke (the author of the article) lives on the island of Bonaire, a small island in the Caribbean. Get your students to share information they have about the Caribbean: *Has anyone been there? What's the weather like? What different languages are spoken there? How many famous people from the Caribbean do they know?*

After reading
- **Important numbers:** There are quite a few numbers mentioned in the text. Once your students have read the text, get them to close their books. They can work in groups. One student from the group can look at the text and ask, for example: *Why is the number 30 important in the text?* If no one can remember, then they can look at the text again. The first person to give the correct answer chooses the next important number.

City break: Hong Kong

Before reading
- Get your students to discuss what they know about Hong Kong and what they would like to know about Hong Kong. While they are reading they can check to confirm their ideas, or, hopefully, get the answers to some of their questions.

After reading
- **Personally … :** Get your students to discuss three things they would like to do in Hong Kong, and one thing that they would not like to do.
- **An indescribable city:** Your students search the text for any adjectives which may describe Hong Kong or some of the features of Hong Kong. Can they apply any/some/all of the same adjectives to their own town?
- **The same but different:** In groups, the students make two lists, one of similarities and one of differences between their home town and Hong Kong.
- **Comparing cities:** As this is the last journal of A2, they may like to compare the cities in the three journals. Have them sit in groups of three, one looking at the Chicago text, one the Istanbul text and one the Hong Kong text. How many similarities and differences can they find?

Ups and downs

Before reading
- Ask your students to discuss two things. Ask: *What is the highest point you have been in your lives, both 1) physically and 2) emotionally.*

After reading
- **Best places:** The students can discuss the best places in the world to live to make you happy. Why are they better than other places?

Journal III

12

At the end of unit 12 your students should:
- have revised the key verbs in the book.
- have revised the tenses introduced and practised in the book.
- have talked about strategies for success.
- have practised giving advice.
- have practised formulating and answering questions.
- have discussed the various members of the class and their talents.

A The keys to success
coursebook pages 122–123

1 Your students match up some phrases to give mottos for personal success.

  1 C   2 A   3 E   4 F   5 B   6 D

Once the students have put the sentences together, they can rank the mottos in terms of how relevant they think they are. They can discuss this with their partners.

2 A vocabulary consolidation exercise in which the students use the key verbs from Key A2 (in the box) to complete the text. Note that they have to use the verb in the right tense and also note so that some verbs appear more than once – in both the box and the text.

1 run	6 is	11 taking
2 spent	7 was	12 moved
3 'll try	8 taking	13 work
4 get	9 look	14 don't have/haven't got
5 put	10 give	15 will never have

The students should note down Sally's four keys to success.

have passion/be passionate   enjoy taking risks
have the right connections   have talent

3 The students discuss successful strategies to help one or two of the four people profiled find solutions to their problems. Once they have debated the issues – and hopefully come up with some ideas – they can get together with other groups to compare notes, orally of course.

4 **2.25** The students listen to Barry and his assistant Janice discussing three more people that Barry might want to feature in a new 'Secrets of Success' interview. Stop the recording a few times to allow your students to choose (and debate) the answers.

	Kieron	Paddy	William
1	✓	✓	
2	✓	✓	✓
3			✓
4	✓		✓
5			✓

6 That is for the students to decide – and discuss.

Matching the motto to the person is again a matter of debate for the students.

Suggested answer:
Kieron: C   Paddy: A   William: B

5 Carrying on with the theme of success, the students need to look back at earlier units to get the answers to four questions.

1 He can speak 12 languages and is a whiz with numbers.
2 He took a fridge with him – and hitchhiked!
3 He films the programmes in his own home.
4 She set up a job-related learning centre in Durham.

The students can now write questions for each of these people. Hopefully they will have plenty of interesting questions. Here are some suggestions.

1 Daniel, how do you start learning a new language? Do you have any tips?
2 Tony, the first question has to be, 'why'?
3 Sam, what do you think of other chefs that have big studios and use exotic ingredients?
4 Jane, do you feel sorry for people who try to buy themselves happiness with fast cars and expensive holidays?

6 And finally … The students interview each other to find out their personal tips on how to be successful. They can begin with one of the areas given and if they have time, they can ask about other areas. There is no answer key as they will come up with their own questions – and answers.

B To tell you the truth

coursebook pages 124–125

1 Your students look back through the book and choose the three images they think are most interesting. They then discuss their choices with their partners.

2 A reading exercise in which the students answer questions about Beth's website.

1	Work	She's a registered nurse.
2	Holidays	She's been to China, South East Asia and India.
3	Lifestyle	She has many different hobbies but her passion is toy making.
4	Dreams and Plans	She's going to visit the Toy Fair in Nuremberg to make new contacts.
5	Talents	She's good at making toys.

3 The students work in small groups to look for information in earlier units and then answer a number of questions about themselves. A model answer is given below.

Model answer for 'Talents'

1 If you can build a hut or find food, you're a good candidate.
2 Three skills are doing magic tricks, juggling and being multilingual.
3 You'll have to climb stairs every day for a month or make the town greener.
4 One is dead, one is a famous TV personality and one chose to give her money away.

4 The students keep the themes they looked at above and write three more questions which they then ask their classmates. They then present the results to the class.

> Use **photocopiable 24** for students to revise vocabulary and phrases from the book.
>
> - Make a copy so that each group of 2–3 students has one card, and cut the cards out.
> - Explain to your students that they are almost at the end of A2 and it is time to look back at the whole book. Also, you enjoy literature and theatre so you are looking for your students to be creative.
> - Explain that all the information they need is explained on the card.
> - They have a maximum of 15 minutes to collect the material and do the writing.
> - They then take turns reading out the texts and acting out their dialogues.

5 And finally ... A lovely exercise at the end in which the students share information that they have learnt about each other during the course. Hopefully they will say nice things about each other!

Notes

Notes

Notes

Notes